Harald Jes

The Terrarium

Setting up and maintaining a terrarium made easy

Expert advice for first-time terrarium owners

With color photographs by well-known animal photographers and drawings by György Jankovics

BARRON'S

Contents

Inside front cover:
*Two African
blue-tailed skinks
in their typical
environment,
recreated in a
desert terrarium
with sand,
stones, and
grasses.*

*To threaten
an adversary, the
bearded dragon bristles the
scales on its throat, which are
elongated in the form of prickles.*

Preface

Fossil finds indicate the ancestors of our terrarium animals were here as early as 350 million years ago. The amphibians and reptiles exert a special fascination, probably because they are so fundamentally different from warm-blooded animals like mammals and birds. Many terrarium residents, particularly the lizards, call to mind the giant reptiles of long-past eras. Although these giant reptiles became extinct over 60 million years ago, their fascination continues.

In easy-to-understand language, terrarium expert Harald Jes explains the biological characteristics of terrarium animals and how those features dictate the type of terrarium to use and the care required. Species accounts of suitable amphibians and reptiles make the choice easier for you, and provide details of the environment and care the animals need.

On the how-to pages, you will find additional tips on setting up and decorating the various types of terrariums, along with guidelines for providing the animals with the best possible habitat and care. You will learn about the Endangered Species Act, and why it is important to follow those regulations. The thorough, hands-on instructions, together with the oversized color photos and informative drawings, make this book a source of invaluable advice for all first-time terrarium owners.

The author of this book and the editors of Barron's series of nature books wish you much pleasure and great success with your terrarium.

Please read the Important Notes on page 63.

3

Understanding Terrarium Animals

In the course of their history, over millions of years, amphibians and reptiles have adapted to their particular environments and developed characteristics appropriate to their habitats.

The Australian giant green tree frog lives on branches and leaves in tropical rain forests.

The Skeleton and Musculature
Skeleton: The skeleton of the amphibians contains comparatively little calcium when compared to that of the reptiles, and the bones of amphibians are usually more elastic. In turtles, the spine, ribs, and portions of the shoulder girdle gave rise to the rigid shell, in which the neck (cervical) and tail (caudal) vertebrae are the only elements that have retained any mobility.

Limbs:
• Tree-dwelling lizards like the striped basilisk and the green iguana can be recognized by their extremely long limbs and sharp claws. The chameleon uses its prehensile tail as an additional "fifth hand." The opposing toes of the chameleons allow them to completely encircle branches (see drawing, page 11) and grip them tightly.
• Ground-dwellers like the leopard gecko and the bearded agama, in contrast, have short, muscular legs, frequently with powerful feet suited for digging.
Reptiles that live in or near water, like the turtles described in the species section (see Popular Terrarium Animals, page 33), usually have webbing between their toes, to assist in swimming.

• Unusual limb adaptations include the suction cups on tree frogs' fingers and toes and the gripping lamellae on the feet of many geckos, which they use to find a foothold even on slippery or vertical surfaces.

Tail: Yet another anatomical adaptation is the ability of many lizards to spontaneously separate their tail, or some part of it, in reaction to danger. This self-mutilation—known as autotomy—serves as a means of self-protection, since an attacker is easily distracted by the cast-off tail. The piece of tail, which has an independent nervous system, continues to make wriggling movements for some time. A new tail is grown in place of the separated one, though it differs in appearance from the original tail.

The Sense Organs
Eyes: The ability to see varies widely among the individual amphibians and reptiles, depending on their mode of life.
• Ground-dwellers like the frogs or toads (called anurans), are predators and can see well, while water-dwelling species like clawed frogs depend more on their sense of smell.
• Terrestrial turtles and tortoises can distinguish colors very well and thus recognize favorite flowers and fruits from a great distance.
• Snakes and many lizards like the chameleon and the knight anole are

The knight anole lives in trees in rain forests.

movement-oriented, and secondarily rely on their sense of smell. Chameleons can move their large, conical eyes, covered with closely joined eyelids, independently of each other. As a result, they can perceive objects behind them and in front of them simultaneously.

• Terrarium animals that become active at night (nocturnal) or at twilight (crepuscular) like tree frogs, toads, leopard geckos, and tokay geckos, have slit-shaped pupils. Thus their eyes, which are adapted to a low level of light, are protected during the daytime. As the light intensity decreases, the pupil dilates.

Special feature: In all snakes, most geckos, and some skinks and lizards, the lids have grown together. They form a transparent "spectacle," or brille, over each eye.

Important: Since they are part of the skin, the spectacles, too, are shed (see Shedding in Snakes, page 46).

Ears: The ability to hear, too, differs widely among the individual species. Snakes and tailed amphibians like salamanders can perceive only earth tremors and vibrations through their abdominal scales and skin. Although reptiles and amphibians generally lack the outer part of the ear, they have an inner ear, protected by skin or an eardrum. The crocodilians have a valve or flap that covers the internal ear during swimming. Frogs and crocodiles, whose voices resound loudly during mating and when marking the limits of their territory, also have the best sense of hearing.

Tongue: The tongue's physical appearance and range of applications vary from species to species.

• Land-dwelling anurans like toads and tree frogs use their tongue to seize prey. The tongue becomes sticky when it passes over the inter-maxillary gland near the roof of the mouth as it darts forward.

• Chameleons have a high-speed tongue the length of their body, thickened like a club at the tip and shaped so as to grasp insects (see drawing, page 11). The length to which the tongue can be extended makes up for this animal's very slow forward movement.

• Most lizards and all snakes use their tongue to seek out their prey. Darting it in and out, they pick up scents, which are passed on to their palate, to the Jacobson's organ. The Jacobson's organ analyzes the odors.

• The tongue of snakes and some lizards is long and deeply cleft; in turtles and most amphibians it is more or less short and thick.

• Many lizards, after eating, clean their mouth at length with their tongue. Almost all reptiles use their tongue to lick up water. Geckos lick their eyes to clean them.

The Skin

Amphibians have a soft, damp skin with a great many glands. The secretion of the glands keeps the skin from drying out. If the animals live in damp surroundings, the secretion also inhibits the growth of bacteria and fungi, replacing the protection supplied by a horny skin.

Not only do amphibians feel slippery to the touch, some of their

The ancient ancestors of some reptiles were already in existence during the era of the dinosaurs.

secretions are poisonous as well; generally the brighter the "warning" colors of the animals' bodies, the more poisonous the secreted substances.

Important: Although all these toxins are not life-threatening to humans, thorough hand washing is necessary after handling.

Reptiles, however, have a dry-feeling, leathery skin without cutaneous glands. This type of body covering, made up of scales of different sizes, some of which are extremely horny, is highly suitable for preventing dehydration, or desiccation.

Shedding

Reptiles: Almost all reptiles, including the turtles, shed regularly. The outer skin quickly becomes too constricting for fast-growing young, so they shed their skin more frequently than older animals. Shedding depends on the season, climate, food supply, and the animal's general condition. Regulated by hormones, it is an especially conspicuous process in snakes (see page 46).

Amphibians: Although all amphibians shed, the process often goes unnoticed.

• Anurans eat their skin as it is being shed—the perfect way of recycling valuable anabolic substances.

• Caudates shed their skin in inconspicuous shreds.

Body Temperature

Fish, amphibians, and reptiles are poikilothermic, or cold-blooded vertebrates, whose body temperature is determined by the ambient temperature. Since all their vital processes are regulated by external factors, terrarium conditions must be controlled to a much greater degree for these animals than for warm-blooded animals.

At a Glance: Amphibians versus Reptiles

Amphibians—Which Animals Belong to This Group?

Tailed amphibians (caudates), such as the axolotl, and tongueless amphibians (anurans), such as the clawed frog.

Distinguishing Marks:

Extremities: Four fingers, five toes
Skin: Copiously furnished with glands, damp, well supplied with blood, no horny scales
Respiration: Through gills, skin, and/or lungs
Reproduction: Eggs are encased in jelly, and have little yolk. Larva generally changes into animal living on land (see Metamorphosis, page 52).

Reptiles—Which Animals Belong to This Group?

Examples include the red-eared slider, leopard gecko, striped basilisk, and corn snake

Distinguishing Marks:

Extremities: Those reptiles with legs have five fingers, five toes (crocodiles: five fingers, four toes)
Skin: Few glands, dry, poorly supplied with blood, horny scales and plates
Respiration: Through lungs
Reproduction: Eggs have large yolks. Young fully developed at birth.

Terrarium Types and Technology

The green iguana, with an overall length of 80 inches (200 cm), is the largest lizard presented in this book.

Location

Basically, a terrarium can be set up anywhere, since the necessary conditions can be created equally well in your living room, a basement, or a conservatory. All you need is the proper equipment.

Size

Always begin by determining how much space you have available for the tank. Then read the species accounts to determine the size and behavior of the animals you're thinking about buying (see Guide to Terrarium Animals, page 34). Most terrariums are about twice as long as wide and roughly equal in height and width. The ratio of length to width to height is approximately 2:1:1, or 28 × 16 × 16 inches (70 × 40 × 40 cm), for example.

Terrarium for climbers: For animals that are tree-dwellers or climb on rocks, such as the tokay gecko and the knight anole, increase the height and alter the ratio to 1:1:2.

Terrarium for terrestrial species: For land-dwellers like the leopard gecko, a shallow terrarium with a ratio of 2:2:1 is best.

Terrarium for aquatic species: For water-dwelling species such as the Chinese fire-bellied toad or water turtles, an aquarium with a ratio of 1:1:1 is suitable.

My tip: As for the rest, there is no need for terrariums to be always rectangular. Corner containers or containers with curved panes could conceivably be used.

Glass or Plastic?

All-glass terrariums are preferable. The plastic terrariums often found on the market scratch so easily that they are suitable at best only for short-term housing of amphibians and reptiles. With a wire-mesh cover that allows light and ultraviolet rays into the container, these models can be employed as breeding and quarantine terrariums (see The Quarantine Terrarium, page 31). Be certain however, not to place the terrarium in direct sunlight; the tank will very rapidly heat up and hold the heat, causing the inhabitants to die.

Air Circulation

A terrarium with solid sides offers little in the way of air circulation. Consequently, you have take steps to ensure adequate air movement in your terrarium.

Aeration: Replace part of one wall with wire mesh, or part of a wall can be perforated. For the greatest amount of circulation, use a terrarium made of wire mesh. An alternative solution is to use wire mesh for an

The clawed frog becomes a lung-breathing animal, but continues to live in the water.

Only in an extremely warm, dry desert terrarium is a spotlight a good choice as the sole source of light.

entire side of the tank, placing the wire mesh opposite the wall where the air intake is located.

The size of the mesh (or the size of the perforations) depends on the size and strength of the animals, as well as the size of their food. Simple physics will help move air through your terrarium; as the air in the terrarium is warmed, it rises and draws cooler air in after it.

Important: Synthetic meshes or screens are not suitable; they can be melted by heating lamps and eaten as food by creatures placed in the terrarium. The larger residents can use their claws to rip their way out.

Doors

A terrarium with paired sliding glass doors on the front will allow you to easily reach inside. The doors should move on parallel tracks. Since you need to open only one half, your escape-minded charges' attempts can be foiled readily. To keep sand and earth from blocking the door, make sure that the tracks run atop a solid front, about 4 inches (10 cm) above the terrarium floor.

Which Kind of Terrarium Is the Right One?

Because of the dependence of amphibians and reptiles on external temperatures, (see Body Temperature, page 7), you have to pay considerably more attention to controlling the enclosure's temperature and humidity than if you were housing birds or mammals. The closer you come to recreating natural living conditions for your terrarium animals, the more suit- able the terrarium is as a habitat.

Tip: The boundaries between the terrarium types described below are fluid, and they overlap in many ways.

The Rain-Forest Terrarium

Extremely beautiful miniature land- scapes can be created in a terrarium of this type, provided it measures at least 28 x 16 x 20 inches (70 x 40 x 50 cm).

Plants: The plants that do well in this kind of terrarium can grow in the bot- tom material or, quite typically, on the walls and on branches of other plants such as epiphytes (see photo, page 12, and drawing, page 19). In choosing plants, take into account the weight and size of the animals (see Guide to Terrarium Animals, page 34).

Places in the sun: For sunbathing reptiles like the knight anole, include plant-free "sunny" spots in your plan- ning. Heat these areas with spotlights (see drawing, page 15).

Plant wall: A plant wall will substantially increase the amount of usable space, because the animals can also live on the back and side walls, provided they are appropriately structured (see HOW-TO: Setting Up, pages 26–27).

Rain-forest terrarium without live plants: If the animals you've chosen are too big and heavy for the plants, or if the lighting can't be arranged to suit both animals and plants at the same time, I recommend a rain-forest terrarium without live plants. It can be made attractive with branches for climbing and other decorative materials (see page 24).

The Desert Terrarium

The typically barren habitat required for a desert terrarium is much more difficult to make attractive. Even without the green of living plants, however, you can create interesting scenes with stones, wood, sand, and dried plants.

Stones: Look around in the mountains or in a quarry. Let Mother Nature show you how rock formations "grow." By structuring the back and side walls skillfully, you can create additional running surfaces, niches, and hiding places (see HOW-TO: Setting Up, pages 26–27). To structure the terrarium floor, use sand and the same kind of stone you chose for the rock backdrop—distributed simply or arranged to create hideouts and sunning areas.

• Don't place stones where they will block circulation!

Wood: Tree roots, dry branches, and dried cactus skeletons, too, can be put to excellent use here. They can be used to organize and subdivide the terrarium, as well as to arrange sunning spots and hiding places.

Sand: Cover the terrarium floor with sand. Apart from giving water to the animals by misting them lightly (see HOW-TO: Care, pages 50–51), you need to keep the sand dry. Cavelike hiding places are exceptions; terrarium animals like to go into them because of their moist, cool floor.

Plants: You can put plants in a dry terrarium too, but only if you can supply them with water without simultaneously soaking the entire floor.

My tip: You can accomplish that, for example, by using stones or a glass strip as a divider, fastened to the floor and walls with glue. Alternatively, you can use plants in separate pots.

Dried plants: Decorating with dried plants like grasses or broom is more practicable, however, especially for novice terrarium owners. Here you can give free rein to your fantasy. A thick piece of styrofoam can be pierced to hold dried stems, then concealed by sand.

The chameleon lives in branches and hunts by using its long tongue like a slingshot.

In a rain-forest terrarium, attractive scenes that recreate the natural habitat can be created.

The Aquatic Terrarium

Although—or precisely because—water is the determining element here, this type of terrarium can be designed in many different ways. The four examples that follow demonstrate how greatly the various design options for water terrariums depend on the habits of their inhabitants.

Aquatic terrarium for water-dwellers: This type of terrarium can best be described as an aquarium with emergent water plants, plants that protrude to varying degrees above the water level. Amphibians that live in water exclusively, like the axolotl and the clawed frog, are the right choices for such a habitat. If the container is filled only with enough water to produce a depth of 4 to 8 inches (10 to 20 cm), you can use climbing plants with water roots (see Table of Plants, pages 22–23), which will keep both the area above water and—with climbing supports—the backdrop green.

Aquatic terrarium with dry places: A much lower water level is necessary in an aquatic terrarium for animals that do not live exclusively in water, such as mud turtles. They need haul-out places, so they can dry off occasionally under a spotlight. These may be structures rising above the water like islands, a protruding piece of driftwood, or a shelf mounted above the surface of the water.

For haul-out places you need to use pieces of perforated plastic, because they will be more durable. If enough room is left above the water, you can include a branch with an epiphytic plant.

Aquatic terrarium with a damp island: Tiger salamanders or fire-bellied toads will find an excellent home in a container with water 4 to 8 inches (10 to 20 cm) deep, a shelf mounted over the water, flat islands made of slate or sandstone, and a profusion of climbing plants. To make the tank even better, cover the island areas with consistently damp peat moss. Climbing plants with water roots need contact with water if they rise above the water, using climbing supports such as osmundum (see HOW-TO: Setting Up, pages 26–27) along the walls and resinous pine roots placed on the container bottom.

Aquatic terrarium with land zones: This version also requires a water level of 4 to 8 inches (10 to 20 cm), but only covering about one-third of the total area. Plants that rise above the water, profuse displays of ground plants and climbing plants in the land portions, and an epiphyte branch up in the air are good subdividers in a tank like this, used to house animals like the tree frog or the garter snake. This type of terrarium needs dry zones as well.

Keeping the water clean: The more water in the container, the more trouble it is to change. If your container holds 13 gallons (50 L) of water or more, it is advisable to install a filter. Even so, you will have to change the water on a regular basis (see HOW-TO: Care, pages 50–51). There is no rule for determining the intervals between changes; you will have to let experience be your guide.

Terrarium Technology

Most terrarium owners almost exclusively depend on animals from tropical or subtropical areas. Equipment that will control the temperature and humidity inside your container is a necessity.

Caution: Since this equipment is operated by electricity, you need to be aware of the dangers involved, particularly those posed by using electrical appliances near water (see Important Notes, page 63).

Heating

Heat radiator for diurnal animals: Since many terrarium animals are heliothermic, and depend on the combination of warmth **and** sunlight you can't simply place the terrarium on top of a heating element. Excellent sources of light and warmth for species such as the green iguana and the Hermann's tortoise are reflector spotlights (see Lighting, page 15), easily obtained at larger hardware stores.

Infrared lamps for nocturnal animals: For crepuscular (active at twilight or before sunrise) and nocturnal animals, as well as those from shadowy habitats (such as the tree frog and the tokay gecko), infrared heat lamps are ideal. These ceramic lamps screw into ordinary light sockets. For large terrariums, area lamps are available (up to 500 watts).

My tip: To keep the animals from being burned, attach all lamps outside the terrarium if possible. Where that is not possible, a wire guard made of mesh is a good idea.

Bottom heating: In ideal circumstances, the heat from the reflector spotlight ought to be adequate. Nevertheless, a source of bottom heat may be necessary as well, if:
• the unheated location of the terrarium means the tank gets too cool at night after the spotlight is turned off;
• in a terrarium without live plants, you want to increase the humidity level through evaporation;
• you want to heat the bottom of a sunning island, to supplement the effect of the spotlight.

Bottom heaters are available in the form of heating cables or heating mats, in various wattages. Less dangerous for the animals are types with relatively low surface temperature, or those that go under the tank. Even if the instructions don't suggest it, for those bottom heating elements inside the tank, be sure to cover bottom cables or mats with wire mesh made of chrome steel (mesh size: $1/8$ to $1/16$-inches or 5 to 10 mm), to keep animals that dig from harming them or changing their position.

My tip: The bottom heating should never heat more than one third of the floor surface; that way, the animals will always have some cooler zones available.

Aquarium heating element: For heating the water in an aquatic terrarium, aquarium heating elements (50 to 300 watts) can be submersed in a perforated clay pipe or hollow rock and thus protected from jostling, bites, and sharp claws.

Caution: Follow the installation instructions for all heating devices with great care (see Important Notes, page 63).

Controlling and Regulating Temperature and Humidity

Only a few tropical regions are warm day and night. Fluctuations of 27°F (15°C) between daytime and nighttime temperatures are no rarity in many regions. The humidity, too, can vary considerably as day and night alternate—hence the term "relative humidity." Good care includes controlling and regulating the climate of your terrarium.

Experience indicates that decreasing nighttime temperatures year-round by 9° to 18°F (5 to 10°C), as well as decreasing daytime temperature in the winter can noticeably boost the vitality and life expectancy of terrarium animals.

Time switches: To control the day-night rhythm, use one of the automatic time switches widely available commercially. It will turn off the lights and heating at night.

My tip: If you work during the day, you can use this technology to alter the day and night periods so that you can observe your pets' activities during the evening hours, too.

Thermometer: To monitor the temperature, you need some kind of thermometer. This might be either a simple model that measures room temperature or a battery-operated digital thermometer. A minimum-maximum thermometer, which shows the highest and lowest temperatures of the day, is a wise choice for terrariums that are exposed to extreme temperature influence from outside, or when you are absent during the day and need to know about possible daytime temperature fluctuations due to power outages.

Thermostat: Use a thermostat to control the heat sources. A great many devices—from simple bimetal models to electronic control mechanisms—are available at a wide range of prices. Thermometers and thermostats with elongated temperature-sensing elements are useful, because they can measure the temperature in parts of the tank outside the zone of the heat sources' direct influence.

Important: These kinds of control instruments are installed outside the terrarium. To keep the lead-in to the temperature-sensing element from being damaged by the animals, run it through a tube or a hose.

My tip: Make temperature comparisons occasionally to make sure the equipment is in working order, because control instruments are not infallible.

Hygrometer: The relative atmospheric humidity is measured with a hygrometer, which, unlike the thermometer, always has to be attached inside the terrarium. It is important to activate the capillary strings in the measuring instrument from time to time (see directions for use).

Regulating the humidity: By watering the plants and dampening the portion of the floor that may be gently heated (see Heating, page 13), you can increase the atmospheric humidity. Constant monitoring is especially necessary after first setting up the terrarium, since it can easily become swampy. If that happens, replace the bottom material (see HOW-TO: Care, page 50).

Don't be surprised if a daytime humidity level of 60% increases to

With an additional spotlight, you can create a sunning spot for warmth-loving animals.

90% or more at night and the panes of the terrarium mist over. The "dewdrops" produced by the declines in temperature are a most welcome source of water to drop-licking reptiles and many amphibians, as well as many plants.

Lighting

Light, together with air and water, is one of the necessities of life. Light is needed in a terrarium as well—and in very large amounts if you plan to keep diurnal animals from tropical or subtropical regions.

Since plants and animals quite frequently have very different requirements for light, you should put only species from the same habitats in your terrarium. When choosing sources of light, there are several types to choose from.

Fluorescent lamps: They make good standard lighting for all terrariums up to a height of 28 inches (70 cm). These double-ended tubular lamps are inexpensive to buy and thrifty in their electricity consumption. Look for fluorescent bulbs with a relatively high proportion of red in the spectrum, because they not only provide the best color for the animals and plants, but they also promote lush plant growth.

Although fluorescent lamps will burn far longer, you should change them after 6,000 lighting hours. Since their light intensity diminishes after that point, the plants in particular will be getting an inadequate supply.

My tip: Buy only lamps that are guaranteed to be splashproof.

Spotlights: They are an excellent source of light and warmth, especially when you already use fluorescent lamps, which give off very little heat, and you wish to create sunning places (see drawing, page 15).

Spotlights are commercially available in the form of reflector lamps or pressed-glass reflector lamps. I recommend that you buy the pressed-glass version, because the very thin glass of the reflector lamps will break at the slightest contact with splashed water. Another great advantage is the fact that spotlights operate without fluorescent lamp ballast (see Mercury-vapor Lamps, below).

These heat lamps are sold in wattages of 25 to 150. With an angle of radiation of 30 to 80 degrees—depending on the size of the intended sunning place—you can create a great many variations.

My tip: Since plants are endangered by the heat inside the cone of light,

sunning places as a rule should be plant-free areas.

Mercury-vapor and metal halide lamps: They are available as tube lamps and as festoon lamps, in wattages ranging from 75 to 2,000; however, they need the fluorescent lamp ballasts required for all gas discharge lamps—components that raise the purchase price, but also increase the light yield. Since these high-pressure lamps shed extremely bright light and give off a great deal of heat, they are recommended only for terrariums with a volume of over one cubic yard (meter).

If enough space is available, these lamps are especially useful for keeping light-hungry reptiles like the green iguana.

UV lamp: Ultraviolet (UV) rays stimulate many biological processes. The medium-wave UV-B rays are important for controlling the calcium metabolism of many animals, while the long-wave UV-A rays affect the formation of pigment in the skin. The short-wave UV-C light, on the other hand, reduces the level of bacteria in the aquatic terrarium. As far as we now know, ultraviolet light is of little or no importance for nocturnal and crepuscular reptiles like the leopard gecko and tokay gecko, or for amphibians.

Caution: To keep the animals from getting burned or developing conjunctivitis, you should very gradually increase the length of their exposure to light from one minute daily to one hour daily, over a two-month phase-in period.

Filtering

In a fairly large water terrarium (with a water volume of 13 gallons [50 L] or greater), it is a good idea to filter the

The axolotl, a water dweller, breathes through gills.

water and, to the extent necessary, to heat it as well. Motor-driven filters in various sizes and power ratings, in some cases with integrated heating, are offered by a number of different manufacturers. To install the unit, follow the manufacturer's directions.

For our purposes, expanded-plastic discs of varying porosity make the best filter material. They can be used for mechanical filtering, with suspended particles being retained, as well as for—to a limited extent— biological filtration.

Water change: Neither mechanical filtering nor biological filtering eliminates the need for changing the water (see HOW-TO: Care, pages 50–51). True, they do lengthen the intervals between changes and keep the water clean as far as the eye can tell, but even clear water can be heavily burdened with nitrogen compounds.

Aeration Equipment

Where it is not possible to take advantage of thermal air flow (see Air Circulation, page 8)—because the terrarium is built into a wall, for example—mechanical aeration is an option. While an ordinary aquarium air pump can be used to provide air circulation for smaller terrariums, ventilating fans, rotor fans, and crossflow blowers provide compulsory aeration in larger containers. All these devices are available in home improvement or hardware stores.

Setting Up the Terrarium

When select-ing plants, remember that their actual origin is irrelevant. What really matters is the type of habitat they require. Nevertheless, many terrarium owners are content only when the animals and plants come from the same natural environment.

Plants in the Terrarium

If plants served only as decorations in a terrarium, plastic plants could fill that purpose just as well. When terrarium animals seek opportunities to climb or look for security in safe shelter, however, being among living green things increases their feeling of well-being.

Light Requirements of Plants

The varying amounts of light required are given in the table of plants on pages 22 and 23, with these symbols: +++—a very large amount of light (1,500–3,000 lx), ++—plenty of light (800–1,400 lx), and +—less light (300–700 lx). "lx" is the abbreviation for lux (unit of illumination).

The Right Selection of Plants

Until it is clear that the animals you choose for your terrarium do not eat a vegetarian diet, do not have particularly sharp claws, and are relatively lightweight—until, that is, you're sure there are no disadvantages to their living in a terrarium containing plants (see Guide to Terrarium Animals, page 34)—you should not even think about selecting plants. Plants with soft foliage, light-green plants, and species with colored leaves are more sensitive than hard-leafed, dark-green plants, which also are less affected by heat and UV rays.

Only relatively few plants are good candidates for inclusion in a terrarium. They may be ground plants, ground covers, climbing plants, epiphytes, or aquatic plants.

Ground plants may have a treelike, shrublike, or low-growing habit (manner of growth). They may also take the form of succulents, with water-storage tissue like that found in cactuses. They draw their nourishment principally from the ground, through their roots.

Ground covers such as grasses, vine runners, and mosses tend to form a dense, extensive growth over the surface. Most develop daughter plants, while others are easy to propagate as slips from the growth tip.

Climbing plants grow upward by twining around trees and rocks, always reaching toward the light. Many form aerial roots, which then take in nutrients and moisture from the water basin of the terrarium. Some are parasites, winding their roots around host plants.

Epiphytes are plants that fasten onto other plants, dead wood, or rocks, and are characterized by very distinct growth forms, as well as by tissue for storing water and nutrients. In addition to orchids, some ferns, and even some cactuses, epiphytes also include bromeliads, which are an especially good choice for terrariums because of their typical growth patterns, their interesting way of life, and their multiplicity of forms and colors.

While cactuses store water in their tissue and orchids have so-called pseudobulbs as storage organs, bromeliads use funnels or cisterns at the base of their leaves as water reservoirs.

My tip: The cisterns should be full of water at all times, since they serve as a drinking trough for many reptiles, and a breeding area for some tree frogs.

Caution: Some bromeliads have extremely sharp spines along the edges of their leaves; however, they will not harm the terrarium animals.

Aquatic, marsh, and floating plants grow constantly under water (submersed) or, depending on the water level, more or less rising above the water or floating on its surface (emersed).

The Planting Medium

Leaf mold and needle mold make the best planting mediums for terrarium plants. For climbing plants, osmundum, or dried tree fern, is an excellent choice (see HOW-TO: Setting Up, pages 26–27).

Hydroponics

Hydroponics—cultivation of plants in water containing dissolved inorganic nutrients—is an easy way to supply plants with water and nutrients. You need to conceal the relatively large-volume containers, however; otherwise, they will look out of place. Since the temperature in the terrarium is higher than the room temperature, you have to check the solution for evaporation on a regular basis.

Watering the Plants

To water terrarium plants, use only clean rainwater or desalinized water, which you can buy or make yourself by means of ion exchangers or osmotic exchangers (available in pet stores). To counteract the bottom material's tendency to become

Epiphyte branches are extremely decorative because of their multitude of shapes and colors.

impacted or marshy, I generally recommend that you use a spray device to supply the plants with water. Spray bottles and misters are available in a range of sizes.

My tip: Match the temperature of the water to the temperature inside the terrarium (use a thermometer to measure it), and never add fertilizer.

Plant Pests

In principle, chemical pesticides should never be used in a terrarium. All you can do is to wipe off aphids, root aphids, and scale insects from the plants with a soft, damp cloth or sponge. In addition, you can try to reduce their numbers by increasing the humidity. In persistent cases of infestation, the only solution is to replace the affected plants.

Bromeliad (Aechmea)

Bromeliad (Guzmania)

Spiderwort (Tradescantia)

Bromeliads (Bromeliaceae)

Mammalaria cactus (Mammillaria)

Euphorbia, or spurge (Euphorbia)

Maranta (Calathea)

Prickly pear (Opuntia)

A Variety of Plants for the Terrarium

For every type of environment there is a selection of typical plants that you can use to create natural surroundings for your terrarium animals and to add decorative accents at the same time. With aechmea, guzmania, spiderwort, maranta, and bromeliads, you can create small rain-forest landscapes. Euphorbia, cholla, sedum, and mammalaria cactus are plants that thrive in a dry terrarium.

Thickleaf (Crassula)

Easy-Care Plants for the Terrarium

Name	Habitat	Location	Light	Height	Remarks
Aglaonema *Aglaonema* species	SE Asia	●	+	Up to 20 inches (50 cm)	Ground plant, herbaceous, small species are especially suitable, easy to propagate
Aloe *Aloe* species	Africa	○	+++	Up to 24 inches (60 cm)	Ground plant, succulent, small species are suitable
Anubias *Anubias* species	Africa	~	+	Up to 12 inches (30 cm)	Grows emersed, put in pot in water
Bird's-nest fern *Asplenium nidus*	SE Asia	●	+++	Up to 24 inches (60 cm)	Epiphyte, don't let root ball dry out, young plants are suitable
Bowstring hemp *Sansevieria* species	Africa	◑	+++	Up to 24 inches (60 cm)	Ground plant, low-growing species are highly suitable
Bromeliads *Aechmea* species	C + S Am	● ◑	+++	16 inches (40 cm)	Epiphyte, firm, only for larger terrariums
Bromeliads *Billbergia* species	C + S Am	● ◑	+++	12 inches (30 cm)	Epiphyte, firm species
Bromeliads *Cryptanthus* species	C + S Am	●	++	2 to 4 inches (5 to 10 cm)	Epiphyte, avoid standing water, not suitable for large, excitable reptiles
Bromeliads *Guzmania* species	C + S Am	● ◑	+++	Up to 32 inches (40 cm)	Epiphyte, avoid standing water, small species especially suitable
Bromeliads *Neoregelia* species	S Am	●	+++	Up to 8 inches (20 cm)	Epiphyte, broad leaf rosette, only for larger terrariums
Bromeliads *Tillandsia* species	America	● ◑	+++	2 to 12 inches (5 to 30 cm)	Epiphyte, grows very well without planting medium
Bromeliads *Vriesea* species	C + S Am	●	+++	Up to 12 inches (30 cm)	Epiphyte, no standing water, small species especially suitable
Ceratophyllum *Ceratophyllum demersum*	Tezw	~	+++	Up to 40 inches (100 cm)	Grows submersed, water level must be at least 4 inches (10 cm), has no roots, grows free in the water
Cereus *Cereus* species	C + S Am	○	+++	Up to 40 inches (100 cm)	Ground plant, succulent, only small species are suitable
Climbing ficus *Ficus pumila*	SE Asia	●	+	Leaves 3/4-inch (2 cm)	Climbing plant, grows better on damp stone, wood, or Xaxim than in soil
Cyperus *Cyperus alternifolius*	Africa	~	+++	Up to 40 inches (100 cm)	Grows emersed, stays small in terrariums, place in pot in water
Dracaena *Dracaena* species	Africa	◑	+++	Up to 80 inches (200 cm)	Ground plant, herbaceous with stem, trim to keep shape, easy to propagate
Echeveria *Echeveria* species	C Am	○	+++	Up to 6 inches (15 cm)	Ground plant, succulent, water with care, rots easily
Euphorbia *Euphorbia* species	Africa	○	+++	Up to 80 inches (200 cm)	Ground plant, succulent, small species are suitable
Ficus *Ficus benjamina*	SE Asia	● ◑	+++	Up to 200 inches (500 cm)	Ground plant, treelike, for larger terrariums, choose small species
Flamingo flower *Anthurium* species	S Am	●	++	Up to 20 inches (50 cm)	Ground plant, herbaceous, small species suitable for terrarium, no standing water
Gasteria *Gasteria* species	Africa	○	+++	Up to 8 inches (20 cm)	Ground plant, succulent, uncomplicated
Green lily *Chlorophytum comosum*	Africa	◑	++	Up to 12 inches (30 cm)	Ground plant, runners also grow hanging, not suitable for large reptiles
Haworthia *Haworthia* species	Africa	○	+++	4 inches (10 cm)	Ground plant, succulent, uncomplicated

S Am = South America; C Am = Central America; SE Asia = Southeast Asia

Tezw = temperate zones worldwide; Trzw = tropical zones worldwide; Suzw = subtropical zones worldwide

Easy-Care Plants for the Terrarium

Name	Habitat	Location	Light	Height	Remarks
Ivy trumpet *Epipremnum pinnatum*	SE Asia	●	+	Leaves up to 12 inches (30 cm)	Climbing plant, usually fairly small, aerial and aquatic roots, easy to propagate
Java moss *Versicularia dubyana*	SE Asia	~	+	Leaves 3 mm	Grows submersed, adheres to wood, rocks, and terrarium floor
Mammalaria cactus *Mammillaria* species	C + S Am	○	+++	Up to 8 inches (20 cm)	Ground plant, succulent, only smaller species are suitable
Maranta *Maranta* and *Calathea* species	C + S Am	●	+	6 to 20 inches (15 to 50 cm)	Ground plant, herbaceous, no standing water
Marigold *Mesembryanthemum* species	Africa	○	+++	Up to 6 inches (15 cm)	Ground plant, succulent, not suitable for large, excitable reptiles
Ornamental asparagus *Asparagus* species	Africa	◑	++	Up to 20 inches (50 cm)	Ground plant, herbaceous, also grows hanging
Peperomia *Peperomia* species	S Am	●	++	Up to 8 inches (20 cm)	Ground plant, avoid standing water, not suitable for large reptiles
Philodendron *Philodendron* species	C + S Am	◑	+	Leaves 2 to 20 inches (50 cm)	Climbing plant, aerial and aquatic roots, small species easy to propagate
Prickly pear *Opuntia* species	C Am	○	+++	Up to 80 inches (200 cm)	Ground plant, succulent, small species are suitable
Pteris *Pteris* species	Trzw	● ◑	++	Up to 40 inches (100 cm)	Ground plant, herbaceous, small species are suitable
Ribbed fern *Blechnum gibbum*	SE Asia	●	++	12 inches (30 cm)	Ground plant, herbaceous
Sedum (stonecrop) *Sedum* species	Asia	○	+++	4 inches (10 cm)	Ground plant, succulent
Sedum *Crassula* species	Africa	○	+++	Up to 24 inches (60 cm)	Ground plant, succulent, not suitable for large, excitable reptiles
Spathiphyllum *Spathiphyllum* species	S Am	●	++	8 to 20 inches (20 to 50 cm)	Ground plant, herbaceous, blooms freely
Spiderwort *Tradescantia* species	S Am	● ◑	++	Leaves up to 2 inches (5 cm)	Mat-forming ground plant, climbing, not suitable for large reptiles
Staghorn fern *Platycerium* species	SE Asia	●	+++	Up to 24 inches (60 cm)	Epiphyte, herbaceous, grows hanging, don't let root ball dry out, for large terrariums
Stephanotis *Stephanotis floribunda*	Africa	◑	+++	Leaves 1 3/4 inches (4 cm)	Climbing plant, needs climbing aids, not suitable for large, excitable reptiles
Sword fern *Nephrolepis* species	SE Asia	●	++	Up to 16 inches (40 cm)	Ground plant, herbaceous, avoid standing water and bottom heat
Tree cacti *Rhipsalis* and *Lepismium* species	C + S Am	●	+++	12 inches (30 cm)	Epiphyte, grows hanging, not suitable for larger, excitable reptiles
Tropical duckweed *Pistia stratiotes*	Trzw	~	+++	Up to 6 inches (15 cm)	Floating plant, water level must be at least 4 inches (10 cm), doesn't tolerate water condensation
Vallisneria *Vallisneria spiralis*	Suzw + Trzw	~	+	Up to 24 inches (60 cm)	Grows submersed, water level must be at least 8 inches (20 cm)

○ = dry; ◑ = semidry; ● = moist; ~ = aquatic plant;

+++ = a very large amount of light; ++ = plenty of light; + = less light (see Light Requirements of Plants, page 18)

Caution: When dealing with plants, always take due care (see page 63).

Suitable Decorative Items

Since the plants, stones, and tree limbs from the native habitat of terrarium animals may be impossible to obtain, you will have to find substitutes from your local pet store, garden center, and your own backyard.

Bottom Material

The substrate you choose will largely determine the humidity in your terrarium: A sand substrate drains rapidly; more absorbent leaf mold and needle mold can trap large amounts of water, which will evaporate evenly when temperatures in the cage are warm. By mixing organic material with sand, you can create a substrate that will be ideal for most terrarium types.

Sand: River sand in various grain sizes looks natural. Builder's sand, sold by the bag in home improvement stores, is also an ideal bottom material.

Dead leaves: Not only do dead leaves offer the animals a place to seek cover, but also keep them occupied in a natural way: A pile of dead leaves from your yard will contain an amazing number of small items that will interest your terrarium inhabitants.

Peat moss: For animals that need high humidity, like amphibians, peat moss makes an excellent substrate material, but should not be kept too wet. Osmundum fern (see pages 26–27), however, even dripping wet, can be used as the substrate in a terrarium housing amphibians.

Decorative Stones

Although for most terrariums you can choose stones of any type and origin, limestone has some restrictions. For those animals that cannot

tolerate water that is too acidic, limestone may not be the best choice.

• Granites often have an interesting color, but are too hard to shape. You'll have to be satisfied with the shape and size of the pieces you find.

• Sandstones and slates are easy to shape, and they are available in a wide range of forms and colors.

• Lava is highly porous, hence relatively easy to work into attractive shapes, but it also gets dirty easily. Moreover, the dirt gets below the surface of the rock. It is also too abrasive to use in tanks with turtles; they will scratch their plastrons on this rock.

My tip: Use lava rock only if it can be easily removed for cleaning.

Shaping stones: Use a hammer, chisel, and, if necessary, a lapidary cutting wheel (see page 63). Wear safety glasses. Stone constructions can be glued together and painted with silicon, epoxy, and synthetic mortar.

Artificial rocks can be modeled out of polyurethane foam or mortar and then coated with epoxy or polyester resin and glass-fiber laminate. If carefully shaped, such pieces can look deceptively authentic.

Caution: These adhesion materials are not altogether harmless; follow the directions for use carefully.

Attractive Woods

Pieces of oak, fruitwood, and vine may have especially interesting shapes, while bamboo and coniferous woods (softwoods) are good for creating typical environments.

Resinous pinewood from marshland: Resinous wood, when obtained from river bottoms, etc., is especially decorative. Unlike most other woods, it will not rot in water. Since it is already waterlogged, it will not need weighing down.

The brown basilisk is a skillful climber.

Stumps: Root stumps offer a growing surface for mosses and plants and supply cover for animals.

Bark: The bark of native trees is also very attractive, though it tends to break easily. Cork bark, from your local plant nursery, is thicker, and it is a good material for building backdrops. To use it in this way, first screw the bark to pieces of lumber, either pieces of 1 × 1s or 2 × 2s, which in turn can be secured on the terrarium sides with silicon adhesive, or Silastic. Fill any vacant spaces between the cork bark and the side of the tank with polyurethane foam to keep food animals from hiding behind the decorations.

Dried or Plastic Plants

Where the light or climate conditions are inadequate for living plants and the terrarium residents are small and not boisterous, dried plants can be used for decoration. For large animals like the spiny iguana, broom and thorny bushes are good for portraying dry habitats. Plastic plants, particularly the vining types, can simply be stapled onto a log or a cork wall, and removed for washing when needed.

HOW-TO:
Set Up

In designing a terrarium, almost anything is possible, provided you follow a few basic rules.

Six Golden Rules of Terrarium Design

However close to nature you want the terrarium to be, don't lose sight of the big picture. Excrement, uneaten food, and the cadavers of food animals and terrarium inhabitants have to be spotted immediately and removed with ease (see HOW-TO: Care, pages 50–51).

• If you keep species that establish territories, arrange the space so that some visual obstructions and prominent elements such as plants, stones, and pieces of wood are available.

• A cavern or hollow should not become a dead end. An animal that is fleeing from its adversary needs a back escape route.

• Stone works, whether in the form of backdrops, caverns, or sunning places, should not be piled up in layers on top of the bottom material. If their own weight is insufficient to keep them in place, you need to fasten them firmly to the floor of the container with silicon adhesive so that they are immovable. Stones that suddenly shift can shatter the panes of the terrarium and harm or even kill the inhabitants.

• Be mindful of crisscrossing branches, intersecting surfaces that are not neatly aligned, splintered stalks and stumps, stacked slabs of slate, and wire meshwork. Animals can get caught in these places and can lose claws, limbs, and tails, or even be strangled to death.

• The equipment that controls and monitors the environment needs to be concealed, yet easy to reach.

Building a Plant Wall
Drawing 1

The best way to decorate a wall, especially in a rain-forest terrarium, is to put in a plant wall. Attach a netting or meshwork made of plastic or chrome steel, with a mesh size of 5 to 15 mm, to a wooden frame of 1 × 2s. Then fasten the frame to the side or back wall with silicon adhesive. Fill the spaces with a mixture of soil and moss or soil and peat moss.

Setting the plants: Slips from climbing plants can be stuck directly into the wall. Vines that are not rooted can be held in place with wire or plastic staples. Arrange the plants so enough light can reach the lower region of the terrarium.

Planting medium for climbing plants: Osmundum, a material composed of tree ferns, offers little in the way of structure but provides a good surface for climbing plants. Glue dry pieces of osmundum to the container walls with silicon adhesive. If the slabs of osmundum are kept damp regularly, they make ideal climbing surfaces for the plants.

My tip: When lining the walls, don't cover ventilation panels.

Creating Hiding Places
Drawing 3

The animals can find places to hide in hollow sections of tree trunks. If a section of hollow log is cut smooth on one side and the cut surface is placed next to the front pane of the terrarium, you can easily observe the goings-on inside it. If there are signs of aggression among the terrarium inhabitants, move the hollow log far enough away from the tank

1) There are various ways to design a plant wall in a rain-forest terrarium. When putting in the plants, remember to leave the ventilation grates uncovered.

2) Since resinous pine from peaty soil does not rot, it lends itself especially well to underwater use.

3) A cavern made from a piece of hollow tree trunk and niche-like hiding places in the rocks.

corner to let animals have a chance to escape their pursuers.

If you decorate the back and side walls with stone, you can create overhangs, niches, and hiding places.

Wood in an Aquatic Terrarium
Drawing 2

Resinous pine from peaty soil is the best possible material to create haul-out areas for aquatic animals such as mud turtles. Since these often-bizarrely shaped trunks, some of which were conserved in damp bogs for millennia, do not rot in water, they are also ideal for underwater retreats.

Planting Epiphytes
Drawing 4

Epiphytes can be planted in the forks of branches, in holes in branches, or on pieces of dead wood. The result will look both decorative and natural, provided you follow a few basic procedures:

• The best choice for planting media are hard, moisture-resistant branches of fruit trees, lilac, or robinia (locust).
• You can hollow out little places in larger branches to use for planting. Simply press the plants into holes in the branches. Use wire or fishing line to tie epiphytes onto smaller branches.
• Remove loose soil from the pot balls, leaving the roots

4) If you bore drainage holes in epiphyte branches, standing water will not be a problem.

intact, and bundle them in moss or some other water-permeable planting medium. Then dampen them well and either tie them to the branches or press them into holes or hollowed-out places in the branches.
• Permeable planting mediums such as moss have a hard time absorbing water again once they have dried out completely. Keep them damp on a regular basis. The water you pour on has to be able to drain well, however, since epiphytes do not tolerate standing water.

Planting the Bottom
If you want to set plants in some part of the terrarium floor, proceed as follows:
• Put in a layer of gravel for drainage about 1¼ to 2 inches (3 to 5 cm) deep. The grain size of the gravel should be 0.5 to 3 mm, the size of aquarium gravel.
• Provide a water basin or drinking pool by placing a container on top of the drainage layer, since the water may occasionally splash over or spill.
• Cover the gravel with wire or plastic netting to keep animals from making a mess when they dig.
• Add a layer of leaf mold or pine needle mold as a planting medium. The layer can be between about 1¼ to 6 inches (3 to 15 cm) deep, depending on the size of the plants.
• Set the pot balls in planting holes of the proper size, as with a flower box. Or set the plants in the holes without removing them from their pots.

Guidelines for Choosing and Buying Animals

A young leopard gecko is fond of seeking out cool, damp hollows.

Where to Get Terrarium Animals

You can purchase animals for your terrarium in a pet store, at reptile expos or from reptile dealers, or from a private individual who breeds them. Captive bred animals are frequently advertised in reptile magazines and club newsletters (see Useful Addresses, page 62). If you come across strange-looking combinations of numbers—such as 1.3; 2.0; or 0.1—in these publications, the numbers indicate the sexes: one male, three females; two males; one female. The males are listed first; the females, second.

How to Decide Which Animals to Buy

Diet: A great many terrarium animals feed on other animals. This is not hard for most people when the food item is an earthworm or a bait fish, but some people are squeamish about offering live animals as food for other animals. If your terrarium dwellers feed on rodents, you may want to offer prekilled items. Frozen mice and rats are available at most pet stores, and, as odd as it sounds, can be stored in plastic bags in your freezer until needed. You need to fully understand the feeding needs of individual species before you stock your terrarium (see Animal Food, page 41). If offering live (or once live) food items bothers you, you can decide to buy only vegetarian species.

Cost: As with any purchase, the cost-benefit ratio has to be right. High prices are not always a guarantee of excellent terrarium animals. Con-

versely, very low prices either indicate an animal not suited to terrarium life, or an animal that is not well.

Appearance: Look at the animal you are thinking of buying. The ribs, backbone, and pelvic bones should not be too prominent. The skin on the torso, tail, and thighs should be only slightly wrinkled.

Eyes: They should not be too deeply set in the sockets, and healthy animals should react to visual disturbances such as hand movements by fleeing, increased wariness, or by offering to bite. The eyes should be free of eye caps from prior sheds. Unshed eye caps can lead to blindness.

• Snakes with a pale white to light-blue tone to their eyes are not ill, but are just in early stages of shedding. During this time they should not be disturbed in any way.

My tip: Don't bring snakes home until several days after they have shed.

Skin: It should be free of boils, pustules, and open, festering wounds, which may be caused by metabolic disturbances, fungus infections, and bacterial infections, all of which are difficult, if not impossible, to eradicate.

• These diseases can cause incomplete shedding in snakes (as can inadequate humidity).

• With lizards, especially those with gripping lamellae on their toes, like geckos and anoles, make sure the skin on the toes sloughs off properly; pieces of skin that remain can occasionally constrict the toe so as to cut off the

It's obvious how the mature leopard gecko got its name.

flow of blood. The unshed skin will also make it hard for the lizard to climb properly.

Shell: The shell should be hard, except in very young turtles and tortoises. For these younger animals the shell should give when pressed very lightly. Older turtles with a soft shell—with the exception of soft-shelled turtles, which have a leathery shell instead of a hard one—are suffering from a calcium deficiency, which requires immediate veterinary treatment and a diet with higher than usual mineral supplementation.

Mouth: It should be closed. Jerky opening and shutting, especially if accompanied by a mucous coating or foam around the nose and mouth, indicates that the animal has a respiratory infection. Deposits inside the mouth, however, are an indication of jaw infections or of disturbances of the digestive tract or respiratory passages (see page 56). All of these symptoms are bad signs.

Caution: If you see any of these signs, don't purchase the animal. And keep in mind that the other animals in such a terrarium are likely to be infected as well.

External parasites: It is essential to check all the animals in a terrarium, since wherever you find one tick or one mite there are certain to be more. A mild infestation is not especially problematic, but you need to take action at once (see page 58).

My tip: Carry out this type of treatment in a quarantine terrarium.

Bites, scars, broken-off tails: Fresh or superficial injuries are not dangerous, but they do detract from the animal's value. Open wounds need to be kept clean until they crust over, and attention from a veterinarian will ensure that infections do not set in.

Aquatic animals like this axolotl should be transported in their element.

Transportation

To transport reptiles, all you generally need is a clean linen sack, big enough for the animal and long enough to tie a knot in the neck. For turtles or fairly large lizards, you will also need a cardboard box (see drawing, page 59).

Amphibians should be placed in a plastic container with padding in the form of damp moss, a damp sponge, or a crumpled and dampened paper towel. Aquatic amphibians need a plastic bag filled with an appropriate amount of water (see drawing, left); the addition of a small clump of aquatic plants will give them something to cling to during transport.

Protection against cold: Reptiles and amphibians can be very susceptible to even short-term chilling. If the weather is below 70 degrees, put small parcels inside your jacket. Transport larger containers in a styrofoam box. If you have a long way to go, use a hot-water bottle to warm the box as well. The water should be at a temperature of 95°F (35°C); you need to keep the temperature inside the styro box between 70° and 80°F.

Caution: Never transport the animal in an open basket, in your hand, or on a leash. Apart from catching a chill, the animal could escape, frighten unsuspecting passers-by, and result in serious legal repercussions for you.

Acclimation

At first, to acclimate the animal and to allow you to learn its behavior and watch for any diseases, keep it in a quarantine terrarium for at least eight weeks. Leave it there longer, if necessary, until it is parasite-free, healthy, and eating properly. Only in this way do you have a chance to observe its behavior, state of health, eating habits, and digestion with any degree of certainty (see Preventive Measures, page 56). The quarantine period is also the time to get a stool specimen for analysis. Such samples are important for determining the state of the animal's health.

Note: You don't need to quarantine amphibians that live in the water, if they are not to be integrated into an existing group of animals. Captive-bred animals from old, parasite-free stock probably don't require quarantine either—if you are certain there is not a possibility of disease transmission.

The Quarantine Terrarium

An empty aquarium, with a lid of wire mesh, can easily be used as a quarantine terrarium. Since it is only temporary housing, half the space recommended in the animal portraits (see Guide to Terrarium Animals, page 34) will be adequate.

Note: Lighting and heating are absolutely essential. Side ventilation is not necessary in all cases; the ventilation provided by the wire mesh top should be enough. The exception is for the true chameleons, which do better in cages with lots of ventilation; plan their quarantine quarters accordingly.

The furnishings can be of Spartan simplicity, but they must be clean, practical to handle, and appropriate for the animal's needs (see drawing, page 31). On the floor, place a foam mat 5 to 10 mm thick. Be certain to keep this mat clean. If properly dampened, it also will ensure the correct humidity for those species that need it. In addition, some animals like to hide under it.

A container of water for drinking or bathing has to be part of the furnishings. Never fill it too far—only a limited amount of spilled water can be soaked up by the substrate.

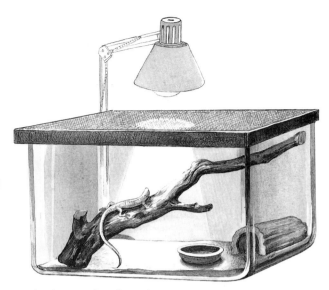

Only the simplest furnishings are needed in a quarantine terrarium.

Compatability: Who goes with whom?

If they are approximately the same size, the following species can be kept together in one terrarium

• the axolotl and the tiger salamander, if there is a land area in the terrarium
• the gray tree frog and the squirrel tree frog
• the Southern toad and the American toad
• the red-eared slider turtle and the snake-necked turtle
• the leopard gecko and the blue-tailed skink
• the striped basilisk and the knight anole
• the garter snake, the banded adder, and the prairie garter snake
• the corn snake, the chicken snake, and the Amur rat snake
• spiny-tailed iguanas of all species

Tiger salamander

Chinese fire-bellied toad

Knight anole

Corn snake

Red belly shortneck turtle

Crevice spiny lizard

Popular Terrarium Animals: A Portrait

The earliest known skeletal remains of a caudate, or tailed animal, date from an era over 350 million years ago. The first reptiles appeared about 260 million years ago, and from them developed the well-known gigantic reptiles we know as dinosaurs, which became extinct 60 million years ago. The finds of the earliest frogs or anurans are 150 million years old. Of these ancient amphibian and reptile ancestors, only the turtles, the crocodiles, and the tuatara have continued to exist almost unchanged until the present time. The ancestors of the approximately 3,000 amphibian species and 6,000 reptile species arose 100 million years ago, during the Cretaceous period. Today their descendants live in the temperate climate zones and are especially numerous in the tropics.

Common garter snake

Green iguana

Climbing surfaces are needed, too. You can use branches, a tree limb, or upended egg cartons, all of which can be disposed of when they get dirty.

Places to take cover can be made with pieces of clay pipe, bark, or egg cartons with an entry hole cut in the side.

My tip: If the new arrival is especially shy or frantic, give it some privacy. Cover the glass side of the tank with paper or cloth, which can be removed bit by bit after a few days, so that the animal can get acclimated gradually.

Care in a Quarantine Terrarium

The animal really should be left undisturbed as much as possible. Carry out only the most necessary procedures, such as:
• changing the water for drinking and bathing; dampening the mat
• removing feces and, if need be, changing the paper or mat. Check the stool, and be sure to send samples for examination at regular intervals (see Diseases, page 56).
• feeding. The animal will wait for a relatively long time before it first eats; for example, turtles wait one week,

Chinese fire-bellied toad.

insect-eating lizards two weeks, and snakes five weeks or more before they start to eat again after joining your household.

Important: When you feed the animal its first meal, don't startle it. Leaves and fruits should be simply placed inside the terrarium, as should prey. Then give the animals time to hunt for their food.

My tip: Don't keep putting the animal in front of its food. Leave it in peace during the acclimation phase.

Guide to Terrarium Animals

The animals introduced here represent only an infinitely small part of the approximately 9,000 amphibian and reptile species that live on the earth. The selection was based on these considerations: We wanted to list amphibians and reptiles that were suitable for a novice terrarium owner, and to present animals with interesting behaviors from different kinds of habitats—especially animals that have proved to be not only easy to keep, but relatively easy to breed in captivity. The possibility of breeding in the terrarium is taken into account, as is reproduction on farms in the animals' countries of origin, because animals born in human care do not have to be removed from their natural habitats.

Regulations for Protection of Endangered Species

This selection is based on the Regulations of the Washington Accord on the Protection of Endangered Species (the Endangered Species Act). Our listing includes only species that are allowed to be kept, bred, and sold.

Washington Accord on the Protection of Endangered Species: This international convention regulates the protection of endangered animal and plant species worldwide. Depending on the degree of their need for protection, various amphibians and reptiles were assigned to protection categories I, II, and III.

Purchase: The amphibians and reptiles offered for sale in pet stores meet the legal requirements for protection of endangered species and may be legally purchased.

Breeding: All the animals presented in this book may be legally bred. However, local ordinances may determine what kinds of animals you can keep, so check local regulations before you get started.

Accountability: If you decide to keep an animal that belongs to a protected species, you may have to prove that the animal was rightfully obtained. The so-called CITES certificate, which serves as a kind of personal identification card, fulfills this requirement. Be certain to keep documentation of your purchase.

Important: Please note that the legal regulations and the protection categories of the individual species are constantly changed and adjusted to the circumstances in the wild. The protection status given here for the animals dealt with in this book was valid as of January 10, 1995.

Criteria Used in the Species Portraits

Protection status: All species listed in conventions or regulations and whose possession or transfer is regulated are designated by the abbreviation "WA" in the following species accounts. Without documentation of their legality, none of these animals may be bought or sold.

Size of the animals: The measurements given in the species accounts are the maximum measurements for adult animals. The head-torso length, measured from the tip of the nose to the vent or cloaca, is significant because of the considerable tail length of some lizards.

Recommendations for feeding: Along with the type of food, we tell you how often the animal should be fed. This information applies to adolescent and full-grown animals. Young animals need to be fed more frequently, but no more than once a day.

Terrarium dimensions: The recommended terrarium dimensions are given in terms of length × width × height. If not otherwise stated, they apply to full-grown animals.

Amphibian Portraits

Axolotl

Ambystoma mexicanum
Photo, page 17; drawing, page 30

Protection status: WA II, exempt from the registration requirement, with the exception of the CITES certificate for export from country to country. No certificate is needed for sales within the United States.

Overall length: 10 to 12 inches.

Range: Central America.

Habitat: Plant-filled bodies of water at higher altitudes.

Behavior: Active in the daytime (diurnal) and at dusk or just before sunrise (crepuscular).

Housing: Aquatic terrarium, with or without land portion, 28 × 16 × 16 inches for two animals.

Decoration: Resinous pine from peaty soil, emersed and submersed aquatic and climbing plants.

Temperature: 64.4–77°F.

Food: Three times a week (daily, for larvae), daphnia, mosquito larvae, earthworms, small pieces of fish.

Needs similar conditions: Clawed toad, *Xenopus laevis;* see photo, page 9; just over 4 inches; tropical Africa.

Chinese Fire-bellied Toad

Bombina orientalis
Photo, page 32; drawing, page 34
   Protection status: S, exempt from the registration requirement.
   Overall length: 2 to 2¼ inches.
   Range: East Asia.
   Habitat: Plant-filled bodies of water with heavily overgrown banks.
   Behavior: Active in the daytime and at dusk or just before sunrise, very social, flees into water.
   Housing: Aquatic terrarium, 24 × 16 × 16 inches, with an island, water depth 4 to 8 inches, for six animals.
   Decoration: As an island, use moss-covered stones or wood; emersed and submersed aquatic and climbing plants.
   Temperature: In the daytime, 68–77°F, at night, 64.4–68°F ; in winter up to 9°F less.
   Humidity: 70 to 90 percent.
   Food: Twice a week (daily, for tadpoles), insects, meadow plankton, small earthworms.
   Special feature: In cooler temperatures they eat much less.
   Needs similar conditions: Tiger salamander, *Ambystoma tigrinum;* photos, front cover and page 32; 10 to 12 inches; North America.

Giant (Marine) Toad

Bufo marinus
Photos, pages 37 and 49
   Overall length: 6 to 8 inches.
   Range: Widespread in the tropics, naturalized in southern Florida.
   Habitat: Tropical rain forests, cultivated areas (e.g., sugar-cane plantations).
   Behavior: Active at night and at dusk or just before sunrise, lives on the ground near water.
   Housing: Semi-aquatic terrarium, 48 × 20 × 20 inches, about two-thirds land, water depth roughly 4 inches, for two animals. A rain-forest terrarium with a dish for drinking water would work as well; Giant toads enter water only for breeding.
   Decoration: Epiphyte branches, climbing plants, which have to be out of reach, however, since they otherwise will be pulled down.
   Temperature: 77°F.
   Humidity: 75 to 95 percent.
   Food: One or two times weekly (daily, for tadpoles), insects, earthworms, baby mice.
   Special feature: Put together only with other animals of the same size!
   Needs identical care: Pixie toad, *Pyxicephalus adspersus;* photo, page 37; 8 to 10 inches, females noticeably smaller; Africa south of the equator; very quiet frog.
   Needs similar care: Berber toad, *Bufo mauretanicus;* photo, page 52; 4 to almost 5 inches; North Africa; lively anuran.

Reptile Portraits

Red Belly Shortneck Turtle

Emydura subglobosa
Photo, page 33
   Overall length: Just over 6 inches.
   Range: New Guinea.
   Habitat: Bodies of water, edges of banks.
   Behavior: Active in the daytime, social animal.
   Housing: Aquatic terrarium, 48 × 20 × 20 inches, with sunning spot.
   Decoration: Island or, even better, wood protruding from the water, large enough to serve as a sunning spot.
   Important: Plants that grow into the terrarium from above have to be kept out of reach, because the turtles might try to escape.
   Temperature: 77°F, sunning area up to 95°F, UV light.

Humidity: 70 to 90 percent.
Food: Three times weekly, daphnia, mosquito larvae, shrimp, small pieces of fish, earthworms, occasionally vegetarian diet.
Special feature: Loves to swim.
Needs similar conditions: Snake-necked turtle, *Chelodina novae-guineae;* drawing, page 38; just under 9 inches; New Guinea.

Leopard Gecko
Eublepharis macularius
Photos, pages 28 and 29
   Overall length: 8 inches.
   Head-torso length: Just under 5 inches.
   Range: Asia Minor, northwestern India.
   Habitat: Dry regions.
   Behavior: Active at night and at dusk or just before sunrise, lives on the ground. In the daytime, seeks out cooler, damp hollows or caverns.
   Housing: Desert terrarium, 20 × 20 × 16 inches, for three animals.
   Decoration: Stone constructions, sand, pebbles, with damp places to hide, dry grasses.
   Temperature: In the daytime, 86°F; at night, 68°F; a constant 68°F during the resting phase from November to February.
   Humidity: 50 to 70 percent.
   Food: Three times weekly, insects and baby mice.
   Special feature: Drinking water is licked off the decorations; spray once daily.
   Needs similar conditions: Rainbow skink, *Mabuya quinquetaeniata;* photo, inside front cover; 12 inches; head-torso length just under 4 inches; Central Africa; savannas, steppes with thornbushes.

Australian giant green tree frog

Marine toad

Pixie toad

Crevice Spiny Lizard
Sceloporus poinsetti
Photo, page 33
Overall length: Slightly over 10 inches.
Head-torso length: Just under 5 inches.
Range: Southwestern North America.
Habitat: Mountains up to 8,200 feet, dry, hot talus slopes.
Behavior: Active in the daytime, lives on the ground, social animal.
Housing: Desert terrarium, 60 × 24 × 24 inches, for six animals.
Decoration: Stone constructions, gravel, dried shrubs.
Temperature: In the daytime, up to 104°F, but the animals have to be able to retreat to cooler zones; at night, 59°F; during the resting phase from November to February, a constant 59–68°F.
Humidity: 50 to 70 percent.
Food: Three times weekly, insects, baby mice, occasionally leaves and flowers as well.

Snake-necked turtle

Special feature: Drinking water is licked up; spray once a day; gives birth to living offspring (viviparous).
Needs similar care: Bearded dragon, *Pogona vitticeps;* photo, page 64; protection status S, exempt from registration requirement; 22 inches; head-torso length, 10 inches; Australia; bush-covered steppes, wooded savannas.

Veiled Chameleon
Chamaeleo calyptratus
Photo, page 57
Protection status: WA II, S.
Overall length: 26 inches.
Head-torso length: 12 inches.
Range: Southwestern Arabian peninsula.
Habitat: Bushland, at higher altitudes also in rare river forests in tropical grassland.
Behavior: Active in the daytime, lives in small branches of bushes and trees.
Housing: Forest terrarium, 40 × 40 × 48 inches for a pair, 24 × 24 × 36 inches for one animal.
Decoration: Branches and leaves that can be gripped by the toes.
Temperature: In the daytime, 77–89.6°F to 59–64.4°F at night; sunning areas, UV light.
Humidity: 60 to 95 percent.
Food: Three times weekly, insects, baby mice, occasionally vegetarian diet.
Special feature: Drinking water is licked up; spray once a day.

Brown Basilisk
Basiliscus vittatus
Photo, page 25
Overall length: 30 inches.
Head-torso length: 8 inches.
Range: Central America.
Habitat: Tropical rain forests, always near bodies of water.

Behavior: Active in daytime, lives in trees, shy, frantic, social animal.

Housing: Rain-forest terrarium, 40 × 40 × 48 inches, for four animals.

Decoration: Climbing branches, stumps, water basin, hard-leafed plants.

Temperature: In the daytime, 77–86°F, 68–77°F at night; sunning places; UV light.

Humidity: 60 to 90 percent.

Food: Three times weekly, insects, small pieces of fish, earthworms, baby mice, occasionally vegetarian diet.

Special feature: Likes to bathe.

Need similar conditions: Knight anole, *Anolis equestris;* photos, pages 5 and 32; 22 inches; head-torso length, 8 inches; Cuba, naturalized in Florida; special features: adhesive lamellae, does not bathe. Tokay gecko, *Gecko gecko;* photo, page 56; 14 inches; head-torso length, just under 7 inches; Southeast Asia; active at night; special features: split pupil, adhesive lamellae, aggressive, doesn't bathe.

With their adhesive lamellae, tokay geckos can cling to any surface.

Giant Green Iguana
Iguana iguana
Photos, pages 8 and 33

Protection status: WA II.

Overall length: 80 inches.

Head-torso length: 20 inches.

Range: Central America to central South America.

Habitat: Tropical rain forests and savanna forests, always near bodies of water, though there are some populations in drier coastal zones.

Behavior: Active in the daytime, lives in trees, bathes occasionally, social animal, though each group has only one full-grown male!

Housing: Forest terrarium, 80 × 60 × 80 inches, for three animals.

Decoration: Climbing branches about the diameter of the lizard's torso, water basin, no plants!

Temperature: In the daytime, 77–95°F (25–35°C), 68–71.6°F (20–22°C) at night, sunning places, UV light.

Humidity: 60 to 90 percent.

Food: Daily, predominantly vegetarian; young animals and some full-grown ones also eat large insects, baby mice, earthworms, and fish. Feed less raw spinach than other leafy green vegetables like romaine lettuce.

Special feature: Can become tame, but always watch out for the claws!

Important: The size this animal is expected to reach and the space it requires mean that potential owners have to look ahead!

Common Garter Snake
Thamnophis sirtalis
Photo, page 33

Overall length: 52 inches.

Range: North America, in several subspecies.

Habitat: Woods, bushland, damp regions, always near bodies of water.

Behavior: Active in the daytime, likes to bathe, catches prey in water as well.

Housing: Aquatic terrarium, 28 × 16 × 20 inches, about two-thirds land, water depth 4 to 8 inches, for three animals.

The white-lipped tree frog reaches a length of up to 4 inches (10 cm) and should be kept in an aquatic terrarium with a land portion.

Decoration: Climbing branches, stumps, emersed and submersed aquatic and climbing plants.

Temperature: In the daytime, 64.4–86°F, 64.4°F at night, during resting phase from November to February, 59–64.4°F.

Humidity: 70 to 95 percent.

Food: Once weekly, fish, earthworms, baby mice.

Special feature: Gives birth to living offspring; peaceable snake.

Need identical conditions: Prairie garter snake, *Thamnophis radix;* 40 inches; North America. Easter ribbon snake, *Thamnophis sauritus;* 40 inches; eastern North America.

Feeding Terrarium Animals

Considering the various feeding habits, we divide our charges into those that eat either a plant or an animal diet exclusively, and those that eat foods from both categories. In the species portraits you will find exact recommendations for the foods preferred by each terrarium animal (see Amphibian and Reptile Portraits, beginning on page 35).

Plant Food

Fruits and vegetables: If grown in your own garden or obtained from a source of organically grown produce, they are highly nutritious. Especially recommended are these vegetables: scraped carrots, with the valuable preliminary stages of vitamin A, as well as spinach and kale, which are rich in vitamin B and minerals. Citrus fruits and peppers are well-liked by terrarium animals, and they are important because of their high vitamin C content. Basically, you should try to buy fruit grown and naturally ripened locally, rather than exotic delicacies, because imported fruits are always harvested before they are ripe.

Rice: Naturally, it will be difficult to obtain all the vegetables listed during the winter months. During this time of year, serving the animals an occasional meal of cooked rice has proved to be a good solution.

My tip: Mix bananas, grated apples and carrots, and unsulfured raisins, dates, and figs with the rice to make the taste more interesting. This rice diet, which can be varied in many ways, is a superb way to include vitamins and minerals (see page 43).

Hay: Hay is also an excellent food. Cut it in small pieces and add it to all the fruit and rice mixtures. You also can make it part of the animals' diet year-round.

Grasses and Weeds

The best nourishment for vegetarians and animals that eat both plant and animal foods consists of all kinds of grasses and weeds found growing wild. Especially suitable are dandelion, plantain, clover, and chickweed, along with all their flowers, of course. However, don't gather fodder plants along heavily traveled roads and streets, near garbage dumps, or in other places that are known to be contaminated by harmful substances (see drawing, page 43).

Animal Food

A majority of terrarium animals are predators, and you need to let them actually eat whole prey. We simply cannot offer predators a diet of hamburger. Apart from that, pure muscle meat is not good for any animal-eating boarder. The skeleton, hair, scales, chitin, and stomach contents of food animals are of great importance nutritionally. Moreover, they are essential to the digestive processes of your wards.

The pixie toad lives in and near water, but buries itself in the ground during the dry season.

Small Mammals

Rats and mice are required items for larger reptiles. You can buy the food animals listed in this book in pet stores or from breeders. Most reptile keepers offer pre-killed rats or mice to avoid trauma to the snake or lizard due to bites.

Aquatic Animals

Freshwater fishes such as common bait fish, trout, and other food fish that can be purchased at pet stores or bait stores, are not only easily digestible, high-protein foods, but also have the highest mineral content. Since they are not always readily available, keep a supply on hand in your freezer.

Daphnia, mosquito larvae, and other small aquatic crustaceans *(Gammarus pulex)* are a valuable food source for small water turtles and water-dwelling amphibians.

Caution: Bodies of water may be leased to someone or protected by conservation laws. Before you try to collect food animals, find out who owns the property and whether it is affected by wildlife conservation laws (see Meadow plankton, below).

Insects and Arachnids

House crickets and other crickets are the most commonly available food insects in pet stores. They are suitable for many animal-eating boarders.

Migratory locusts are good only for larger terrarium animals.

Fruit flies are important items in the diets of young reptiles and of amphibians that do not grow very large. During the summer months, fruit flies can be lured with fruit. Otherwise, you can get them from your local pet store.

Meadow plankton is a generic term for insects and arachnids that you can catch yourself by scouring weed-filled meadows and field boundaries with a stripping net. They are certainly the most natural food you can provide to your insect-eating wards. By the way, the fodder plants you find in such habitats are very likely to be virtually free of harmful substances.

Caution: Don't gather meadow plankton in protected areas, and make sure there are no protected species among the "prey." For information about wildlife conservation regulations, contact your local community or municipal authorities.

Aphids are the easiest type of natural food to obtain, and they are excellent for feeding small amphibians and reptiles.

Slugs, Snails, and Worms

Slugs and snails are popular with many terrarium animals that eat a mixed diet of plant and animal foods.

My tip: If you gather slugs and snails during the growing season, you can store them for several weeks in your refrigerator at a temperature of 41–50°F (5–10°C).

Earthworms, owing to the soil contained in their stomach, are important sources of minerals. You can pick them up, dig them out of the ground, or buy them in stores that sell fishing supplies.

Canned Food

Canned cat food has proved to be a good supplement for many animal-eating terrarium boarders and those who eat a mixed diet. It is also rich in vitamins and minerals.

Important: Don't feed canned food routinely to the terrarium animals, however. Even those that eat animal foods exclusively need a healthful diet with as much variety as possible.

Vitamins and Minerals

Vitamins set in motion vital metabolic processes. They are either ingested as part of the diet or produced during certain digestive processes.

Minerals such as calcium, phosphorus, and magnesium are used primarily for building bones and teeth. Young animals that are still growing especially need to be supplied with them. Trace elements like potassium, iron, iodine, fluorine, and selenium are important for the formation of enzymes and hormones.

Since under terrarium conditions vitamins and minerals cannot be ingested or produced in the body, in sufficient quantities, they have to be added to the animals' diet. If there are clear signs of nutritional deficiencies—such as swelling of the eyelids and metabolic bone disease (see page 59)—vitamin and mineral supplements can be administered directly.

Vitamin and mineral preparations for terrarium animals are available in the form of drops or powder in pet stores, and as multivitamin supplements in pharmacies or from veterinarians. The veterinarian will also tell you how much to use. Drops are trickled directly into the animal's mouth (see drawing 1, page 50). The powder should be mixed with food. Follow the directions for use closely.

My tip: Eggshells or cuttlebone, the internal shell of a cuttlefish, can be crumbled and sprinkled in small amounts into the terrarium each week. Many lizards and turtles will eat the pieces greedily.

Watering Animals

All the amphibians, turtles, and garter snakes presented in this guide are housed in aquatic terrariums and, if need be, provided with drinking water—one more reason to change the water regularly. Rain-forest terrariums have to be misted daily in any event, and the "dewfall" is used by the animals as a source of drinking water. With all other reptiles, the water basin that is part of the furnishings serves as a bath and a drinking trough.

When to Feed

Food always should be served during the animal's activity phase—at its beginning, if at all possible (see

Grasses and weeds that grow wild are especially tasty treats.

Amphibian and Reptile Portraits, beginning on page 35). If the terrarium has its own rhythm, regulated by an automatic switch, you should take that into account, of course.

How Much to Feed

Ask for advice when you are purchasing foods, and keep a close eye on the terrarium to see how much the inhabitants are eating. The right amount of food is however much they eat avidly when fed. Anything more is too much; the animals aren't meant to eat constantly.

Important: Don't feed snakes during their shedding phase.

How to Feed

Moist foods like small pieces of fruit, vegetables, and rice, as well as canned cat food, should be served in bowls. The bowls should be shallow enough to allow the animals to reach the food, but heavy enough that they won't tip over.

My tip: Supplement this type of food with vitamins and minerals.

Baird's rat snake is easy to keep in a terrarium.

Leaves, grasses, and hay are simply placed on the terrarium floor. Make sure to avoid the area where the animals tend to defecate and urinate.

Food animals should not be put into the terrarium until you are completely certain about the species as well as the size of the preferred prey. Consult reptile and amphibian information sources, observe your animals, and try a few samples first. Then you'll be sure that the creatures to be used as food aren't going to escape, but will be speedily caught.

My tip: Since the consequences of dealing incorrectly with live creatures can be fatal, always watch your charges while they eat—food animals have been known to nibble at terrarium animals. Consider using only pre-killed mice and rats.

Note: If several animals are being kept in the same container, it is safer to hold out the prey in front of each one, using tweezers. That will prevent them from fighting over food at mealtime.

Food fish, in sizes that are easy to swallow, should be placed live into the water, where predators can get hold of them and gobble them up. Don't prepare small pieces of fish in filet form; instead, serve them with all their scales, bones, and entrails.

Important: All food removed from the freezer needs to be thawed slowly and served only when it has reached room temperature.

Insects can be dusted easily with a powdered mixture of vitamins and minerals (see page 43): Put a small amount of the mixture into a jar or a plastic bag, place the insects in it, close it well, and shake until the food animals look like they're covered with flour. Then toss them into the cage one by one, so that the predators can catch them after a short hunt. Alter-

Young corn snakes. Like the Baird's rat snake, this species is a native of North America.

natively, handle them with tweezers, holding them in front of the recipient so that they can't escape.

Important: Take uneaten insects out of the terrarium again, since they can harm the animals and plants.

Meadow plankton should be placed directly into the terrarium. Because the climate is different, the creatures won't try to settle in there.

Aphids should be presented along with the leaves and stems.

Earthworms, snails, and slugs should be served under your supervision, because they will hide and be lost as a source of nourishment.

Note: In fairly large numbers, escaped snails can become a danger to the plants!

Feeding in an Aquatic Terrarium

Terrarium animals that live in the water should be given both live and dead food in the water. Take special care not to overfeed these animals, since all excess food will spoil the water.

Forced Feeding

If a terrarium animal refuses to eat for what seems like an unusually long time, it is essential to consult an experienced terrarium owner before you resort to force. Hard and fast rules for acceptable fasting times are impossible to formulate, since these periods are immensely different in length, ranging from two weeks to two years.

With lizards and snakes, there is a relatively large chance of opening the mouth and inserting food (see HOW-TO: Care, pages 50–51). Forced feeding of turtles and amphibians, on the other hand, requires so much skill and entails so much stress for the animals that novice terrarium owners shouldn't even attempt it.

The Right Care

The care of terrarium animals involves not only a great deal of compassion, but also a willingness to learn from experience. Watching attentively and correctly interpreting what you see are fundamental to keeping animals in a terrarium. In short: Observation accounts for fully 50 percent of your task as keeper.

Four Important Rules of Care
1. Scrupulous care and hygiene not only promote good health in the animals (see Diseases, page 56), but protect you, the keeper, as well. Basically, however, there is no direct threat of infection in dealing with terrarium animals.
2. Don't work in the terrarium more than is necessary; any excess activity will disturb the animals. You will see the animals grow less shy as they become increasingly acclimated;

still, every disturbance causes stress.
3. Whether you own one or several containers, keeping the surrounding area clear will make care procedures easier and help you avoid problems and accidents.
4. Always close the terrarium doors and top carefully. Animals that escape have no chance of survival outside the terrarium. Moreover, they frequently cause fear and panic.

Skin Care
The care required by terrarium animals' bodies is not comparable to the grooming necessary for the coats of dogs and horses. Here, instead, you have to make sure that shedding occurs and proceeds in a normal way. Only in amphibians does the shedding process entail no complications.

My tip: To become familiar with the shedding behavior of your lizards and snakes, record everything you observe.

Shedding in Snakes
Depending on the species and age, the skin loses its sheen several times a year, though the change

The food dish has to be sturdy, so that powerful animals like the green iguana can't overturn it.

will be almost unnoticeable at first. Then the colors begin to grow dull, until the snake looks light blue, grayish, or whitish. This change, which is completely normal, is easiest to detect in the eyes.

After four to seven days, the entire snake, including its eyes, becomes brighter in color again, and after another three to five days it will begin to shed its skin. To do that, it rubs and scratches its lip scales on solid objects and thus loosens the skin, which begins at the mucous membranes of the mouth. After the initially exhausting process of shedding the skin on the head, especially around the eyes, the rest should go much faster.

Garter snakes slip out of their skin lengthwise—then you'll find the cast-off skin in your terrarium. Giant boas roll the skin from their neck down over their body, the way you roll a stocking off your leg.

Caution: It is very important that the skin of the eyes, the "spectacles," be shed completely. Any unshed skin can result in eye diseases.

Shedding problems: If the skin is cast off in shreds, there may be a problem. Try to find out the cause of the problem and eliminate it.

Causes of problems:
• The air in the terrarium is too dry. Spray water in the terrarium.
• There may be developmental or metabolic problems. Ask an experienced terrarium owner or a veterinarian.
• Stress may have been caused by a change of location. What to do? Let the animal get some rest.

Direct help: Put the snake in a few inches of water in a bucket or plastic jar, covered with a perforated lid, for several hours to let its skin soften. In most cases the skin will be cast off in

In snakes, shedding starts with the casting off of the skin on the head.

the water. If this doesn't work, try something else (see pages 50–51).

Shedding in Lizards
Lizards shed their skin in shreds. The process is so prolonged in some species that it is starting again on the head just as it is finishing at the tail.

Shedding problems: Lizards, too, occasionally experience shedding problems. Keep a close eye on them.

Causes of problems: In addition to the causes listed in the section on snakes, the following affect lizards as well:
• Other members of the same species may be aggressive, causing stress. Separate the aggressors.
• The terrarium may be overpopulated. Keep fewer animals there.

Direct help: Here you can help by misting the lizards repeatedly with water, three times a day at least, and removing the softened shreds of skin with tweezers.

Proceed with care so that your efforts don't become a source of stress.

Shedding in Turtles
Land turtles, or tortoises, lose skin in shreds, usually when they take an occasional bath.

As a terrarium owner you take animals into your home, but you are not dealing with domesticated pets; they are wild animals, and as such they don't like to be petted, but they do require a serious commitment on your part.

Water turtles have no problem at all with the shedding process. Many species also cast off the top layer of the horny carapace.

Claw Care

Unless climbing lizards are equipped with adhesive lamellae on the underside of their fingers and toes, they need long, sharp claws to keep their footing wherever they go. If the claws of terrestrial lizards and turtles are overly long and curved, however, they have to be shortened. In addition to sand or leaves, put a stone slab, for example, in your terrarium: Insufficient abrasion, along with a lack of activity, is responsible for excessive claw growth.

Trimming the claws: You can use sturdy nail clippers to cut the claws. Make sure you clip off only the extra length; don't cut into the part of the claw where the blood vessels are.

My tip: Beginners should have a veterinarian, pet store dealer, or experienced terrarium owner show them how to perform this procedure.

Picking Up and Holding Terrarium Animals

In some cases you will be forced to pick up one of your animals and hold it quite firmly. That is not always easy, because some are slippery, and most are quick, and well prepared to fight.

Amphibians living in water: Catch them with as large a dip net as you can comfortably use in the enclosure. If you need to hold them firmly in place, that, too, is best accomplished in the net, because the fabric netting makes them easier to grip.

Amphibians living on land: Either catch them with the dip net and hold them firmly in place, or grab them from above just in front of the hip.

Check-up for Vacation

By lowering the temperature (see Technology, page 13), you can induce a pseudo-resting phase and greatly slow all the vital processes in the terrarium. Nevertheless, you have to find someone reliable to substitute for you during your absence, and that person needs thorough training in advance. You can make vacation-time terrarium maintenance easier in these ways:

• Lowering the temperature by about 9°F (5°C) will slow many vital processes. Turn off all the heaters and spotlights; leave on only the light required for the plants. Then the animals will eat little or nothing, and as a result the terrarium will stay much cleaner as well.

• Make sure that the sun's rays don't fall on the terrarium and heat it up. Then not only the animals, but also the plants would need substantially more water.

• Because having to change the water usually is the biggest burden for your vacation replacement, you should reduce the appetite of water turtles that are big eaters by lowering the temperature two weeks before your departure. Clean the terrarium thoroughly the day before you leave, then don't feed the animals again. Also, start feeding amphibians in a water terrarium reduced amounts two weeks before your vacation. Then there will be fewer droppings, and the water won't have to be changed while you are away.

• Spare your substitute the trouble of giving the animals vitamins and minerals.

The marine toad is used to combat pests in tropical countries.

Turtles: Take hold of the shell. Be careful with individuals that bite. If they bite, grasp the shell in the area of the hind legs, so that even long-necked species can't reach your fingers.

Smaller lizards: With the thumb and index finger of one hand, quickly and deftly grasp the neck of a small to medium-size lizard from above. From the sides, hold the head securely in place. Put your free fingers around the animal's body.

Large lizards: Put one hand around the neck and the other around the base of the tail and the hind legs, which are attached at either side of the tail. Keep the animal in place with its hind legs stretched out behind it.

Unruly lizards: If a large lizard is putting up a fight, put the hand surrounding the neck around the front legs as well, because thrashing, sharp-clawed feet can inflict severe wounds. If strong resistance is being offered, you have to take into account the vigorously lashing tail, which not only can injure you, but harm the animal itself as well.

Important: Proceed cautiously with smaller species, such as geckos, that can cast off their tail (see Skeleton and Musculature, page 4). Surround the tail very gently with your hand.

Snakes: Snakes can be seized and held in much the same way as lizards, only in this case you have to deal with a long, writhing body. In contrast to lizards, which usually take flight, snakes take up a defensive position and can bite your hand faster than you can get it around their neck.

My tip: Cover the snake with a cloth to disorient it, and hold it with the cloth.

HOW-TO: Care

Be as careful as possible when carrying out the necessary procedures for cleaning the terrarium and taking care of the animals, in order to avoid exposing them to needless stress. Always do the cleaning first, then attend to the animals.

Cleaning Equipment

For routine cleaning tasks you need a scoop, trowel, tweezers, sponge, brush, and chamois cloth, all of which have to be cleaned thoroughly after every use.

Important: If you use the same utensils for several terrariums, they have to be very thoroughly disinfected before you go from one container to another, because the risk of infection and transmission of parasites differs among the various species of animals.

Caution: Any disinfectants you use have to be water-soluble and easy to remove in running water, to keep the animals and plants from being harmed by traces that remain. Never use any sort of Lysol or Pine-Sol disinfectants; they and their odors are harmful to terrarium inhabitants.

Daily Upkeep

• Remove feces and urine. If the droppings were deposited on the terrarium floor, use the scoop or trowel to remove the dampened bottom material

1) Hold a turtle this way to give it medicine.

under them as well. At the same time, check the consistency of the stool (see Diseases, page 56).
• If excrement was deposited in the water basin, change the water completely. Otherwise, just add fresh water to the basin.
• Smooth any areas that have been churned up.
• Remove uneaten food. Never serve leftover food to animals in another terrarium; that could spread infections.
• In a rain-forest terrarium without plants, mist water to keep the air humid.
• Water or, even better, mist the plants (see page 19). Remove dead leaves.

My tip: Always mist at the beginning of the activity phase (see Amphibian and Reptile Portraits, beginning on page 35), so that both plants and animals are refreshed by the "dewfall."
• Clean the panes of the terrarium. During the acclimation phase, however, clean them only if they are really badly

soiled, since washing the panes disturbs the animals and causes stress.
• Feed the animals as required (see page 44).

Changing the Bottom Material

When the initially fresh scent of earth is replaced by an unpleasant "odor," it is high time to replace the bottom material. Depending on the depth to which the container is filled, the bottom material may get dirty deep down, or it may become swampy because of excessive watering or spills from the water basin. If that happens, remove all the material and replace it with new substrate (see page 24).

Temporary housing for the animals: If extensive work in your terrarium is required—such as replacing the bottom material or putting in new decorations and plants—the animals have to be quartered elsewhere for the duration (see Picking Up Terrarium Animals, page 48). You can use the quarantine terrarium as temporary housing.

My tip: For a few hours, a dark, escape-proof cardboard box is better than a small, bright terrarium, in which the animals will wander around disoriented.

Changing the Water

As soon as the water in an aquatic terrarium is soiled with feces or leftover food, it has to be changed. To do so, use a length of hose to syphon the water into a bucket. Fill the hose with water, close both

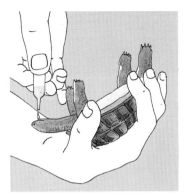

2) Hold the head of large reptiles in place, while the body is in the bag.

ends with your thumbs, hold one end in the terrarium basin and the other in the lower bucket, and then remove both thumbs at once.

Once all the dirty water has been removed in this way, add the fresh water.

Note: For reasons of hygiene, under no circumstances should you suck one end of the hose to get the water flow started.

My tip: Use a thermometer to determine when the new water has reached the customary temperature.

Holding the Animals in Place
Drawing 1

For turtles: To give a turtle (vitamin) drops, hold the animal on its back and place the drops on the tip of its chin. From there they will trickle down between the horny edges into the mouth.

For snakes and lizards: To treat a sick animal—by administering a medication, for exam-

ple—put the animal in a linen bag with only its head sticking out. Put one hand around the bag and the animal's neck, while the rest of the wriggling reptile remains in the bag.

Caution: Despite all your caution, sharp claws can inflict dangerous scratches, even through the cloth. If you are injured, see your doctor (see Important Notes, page 63).

Forced Feeding
Drawing 2

If a lizard or a snake has to be force-fed (see Forced Feeding, page 45), hold the animal in place by putting the thumb and forefinger of your left hand at the sides of its head. If the lizard is small, surround its body with the free fingers of your left hand. Larger lizards as well as snakes can be placed in a linen bag (see above). If fear or a desire to resist causes the animal to open its mouth, you can insert a wooden spatula or, even better, a vaginal speculum (an instrument used by veterinarians) into the oral cavity. If the mouth remains closed, you will have to use your free right hand—or ask a helper—to exert constant pressure on the mouth until it opens wide enough to admit the spatula or the speculum. Next, carefully introduce the appropriate food—no more than 10 percent of the usual quantity—along with some water to help it go down. Administering multivitamin drops at the same time will have a positive effect on digestion. Some European terrarium

3) With your thumb and index finger, hold the snake's head in a pincer grip.

keepers add a dose of boviserin, a serum obtained from the blood of cattle, but this procedure is not commonly followed in the United States.

Repeat the feeding procedure weekly, if necessary. Offer different foods on a frequent basis, to stimulate the animal's appetite.

Helping Snakes with the Shedding Process
Drawing 3

If the "softening" method described earlier fails to provide a complete solution to your snake's shedding problems (see page 46), you will have to intervene directly.

With a gentle grip, hold the snake's head firmly between your thumb and index finger. Then, holding your other hand firmly around the reptile's body and exerting gentle pressure, let it wriggle through your hand. That should help it cast off its old skin.

Breeding Terrarium Animals

How Amphibians Reproduce

Excellent living conditions are required if you want to trigger the reproductive cycle in your amphibians. Often, the length of the day, the climate, or even changes in the climate—a thunderstorm, for example—will act as a catalyst.

Note: Success may depend on your keeping several individuals of only a single species in a terrarium, so that a true choice of partners can be made.

Sex Characteristics

Determining the sex of terrarium animals is difficult, even for experts, because the differences often are perceptible only during the reproductive phase.
• Among most amphibians, the females are bigger and stronger.
• Among male caudates, the cloacal area is greatly enlarged.
• Some male anurans can be identified by their darker throat, the resting sound sac. Others are characterized by horny, usually dark-colored estral calluses on their arms, hands, or fingers.

Spawning Behavior of Caudates

Most caudates seek out water when it is time to spawn. During the courtship stage, the male deposits the spermatozoa in the form of a capsule—the spermatophore—at the bottom of the water, where the mass is picked up by the cloaca of the female. Soon thereafter, the female deposits

The Berber toad is a lively anuran native to North Africa. Its camouflage color indicates its habitat.

the eggs, often numbering several hundred, on aquatic plants.

Spawning Behavior of Anurans

For the most part, the males straddle the females, clinging to their back (see drawing, page 55). As they swim in the water, the eggs are deposited and fertilized at the same time.

From Larva to Amphibian

All the amphibians described in the species portraits deposit gelatinous eggs with very small yolks in the water, from which gill-breathing larvae hatch one to four weeks later. The small, globular beings with their long tails, which in the order of frogs and toads are known as tadpoles, eat constantly and grow relatively quickly.

Metamorphosis: After a few more weeks, metamorphosis begins: the process of transformation by which the water-dwelling larva becomes a terrestrial animal. Among caudates, the front legs develop first; among anurans, the hind legs are the first to appear. Along with their diet, their dentition changes, and the gills regress. Externally there is no sign of the development of the lungs and the changes in the digestive tract, but the tail of anurans can be seen to dwindle. Once metamorphosis is complete, after four to six weeks, most leave the water as fully developed amphibians, to live predominantly on land.

Crevice spiny lizards are social animals from dry, hot environments.

Exceptions: One of the numerous exceptions among the caudates is the axolotl, which continues to breathe through gills and does not leave the water. Among the anurans, one exception is the clawed frog, which goes through a complete process of metamorphosis—that is, becomes an animal that breathes through lungs—but does not leave the water.

Note: Eggs deposited in an aquatic terrarium should be kept in a separate small aquarium, since the burden of the disintegrating eggs as well as the increased feeding of the larvae would be too much for the water.

My tip: Use the dip net to transfer eggs floating in the water to the rearing aquarium. Transfer eggs deposited on plants along with the plants. To maintain the water quality, run the filter intensively and change the water often.

How Reptiles Reproduce

Among reptiles, too, males and females are often hard to tell apart.

With a probe, experienced terrarium owners can detect the sacs of the hemipenis (see Mating, this page) between the cloaca and the tail in some lizards and snakes.

Sex Characteristics

Turtles: Sexually mature turtles are the easiest to identify. In the males, the ventral shell is pitted, the tail is longer and heavier, and the cloaca usually is located farther from the onset of the tail than in a female animal.

Lizards: Most male lizards have more or less prominent crests and skin flaps on their head, throat, back, or tail. Many are also larger than the females. Gender-related skin glands are clearly visible in male geckos and agamas. Sexually mature male iguanas often can be recognized by the base of the tail, which is markedly larger and bulgy underneath.

Snakes: As a rule, male snakes are somewhat smaller. Often the base of their tail is larger, and occasionally the tail is somewhat longer as well.

Courtship Behavior

During mating season, you can observe a great many different forms of courtship behavior among reptiles that are active in the daytime.
• Male land turtles pursue and harass the females, emitting loud cries.
• Water turtles are ardent, rough lovers, and it may well become necessary to separate the animals for the protection of the females.
• During courtship, some lizards display their throat pouch, nodding their heads, while others make rapid nodding and bobbing motions with their head.
• Even snakes develop unsuspected activities where preservation of the

species is concerned, with several males often pursuing the same female.
• Male reptiles, which live together peaceably most of the year, can be extremely aggressive during mating season, pursuing, biting, and even killing one another.

My tip: During this time, observe your terrarium animals even more closely, and separate the combatants at the first sign of aggression. You can use the quarantine terrarium for this purpose.

Mating

The sex organs of all reptiles are found in the ventrally located cloacal cavity. Turtles and crocodiles have a penis with a seminal channel, while lizards and snakes have a two-part (paired) hemipenis. Because of anatomical circumstances, only male turtles mount during mating, while male snakes and lizards approach the females from the side and try to place their cloaca as close as possible to that of the female. The part of the hemipenis that is nearest to the female becomes erect. To ensure a secure connection, the hemipenis is furrowed and equipped with "barbs" and "spikes."

Oviposition

Turtle eggs are hard-shelled, while lizards and snakes lay soft-shelled eggs. Only a few geckos, such as the tokay gecko, produce hard-shelled eggs. As a rule, the eggs are laid in the ground, where the bottom material has the required moisture. In some cases, female tokay geckos lay their hard-shelled eggs in clefts in wood or fissures in rock as well.

Using an Incubator

The eggs should be transferred into an incubator. For one thing, the temperature and humidity inside the terrarium usually are inadequate, and for another, there is a risk that adult reptiles will dig up the eggs and harm them, or pursue the newly hatched young and eat them.

Incubators for reptile eggs are available in pet stores. An old, disused aquarium, in which a fluorescent lamp or a heating cable with a thermostat is installed to guarantee a constant temperature between 78.8 and 86°F (26–30°C), is just as good for this purpose, however. You should transfer the sensitive eggs immediately after you discover them.

• First, fill a closable plastic container half full of dampened vermiculite (available in pet stores).
• With one hand, gently bed the eggs in the layer of vermiculite. Then cover with another layer of vermiculite about ¾ inch (2 cm) deep. Don't cover the hard-shelled gecko eggs.
• Then close the container, remembering to leave a few 2-mm air holes, and place it in the incubator.

Caution: Don't turn the eggs, because the embryo is fixed in place and would be choked by the yolk if the egg's position were changed.

Live-bearing Reptiles

Oviparity is the term used for the form of reproduction described above, involving production of eggs that hatch outside the female's body. Viviparity is the term used for the development of the embryo in mammals, inside the body of the mother. In between there are a great many other types of development in which the embryo, though supplied in a variety of ways by the mother's organism, has no connection to her bloodstream.

Turtles generally are oviparous. Among live-bearing lizards and snakes (e.g., garter snakes) the young hatch from the egg membrane before, during, or immediately after oviposition.

Raising Young Reptiles

Young reptiles are not cared for by the mother or father. Not infrequently, young reptiles are even in danger of being eaten by their parents. Consequently, they need to be raised apart from their parents, but under the same conditions as the mature animals (see Amphibian and Reptile Portraits, beginning on page 35). The food animals, however, need to be correspondingly smaller and the vegetarian foods somewhat softer.

To rear young reptiles, all you need is a plastic or glass container that you cover with gauze. Under no circumstances should the temperature in the rearing terrarium be higher than that of mature reptiles. The young do not need more warmth than their parents.

During mating, the male anuran straddles the female.

The Most Common Diseases

The tokay gecko comes from Asia, where it also lives in human settlements. In the evening it emits loud calls: "To-ke, to-ke."

Preventive Measures

Quarantine: Quarantine is of great importance because terrarium animals on the way from their accustomed environment or their place of birth to you are subjected to many stresses and potential risks of infection. In addition, in a quarantine terrarium you have a better opportunity to observe new animals closely.

Observing animals closely: Observing does not mean simply being on the lookout for pathological changes, but also taking note of behavioral changes. Because the customary reactions of a new animal are not yet familiar to you, you should consult an experienced terrarium owner.

Noting behavioral changes: Keeping a daily record of all behaviors, including eating and digestion, is helpful. The temperature and humidity data, too, can help you draw important conclusions.

Exchanging experiences: Address questions to one of the reptiles and amphibian magazines, or to a local herpetology club. You can ask your veterinarian for analysis of the stool samples, which you should continue to submit on an annual basis.

Important: Don't do any experimentation yourself, since nonspecific or even improper procedures will waste time needlessly. Under no circumstances should you continually give the animals small doses of medications as a preventive.

Stool Changes That the Eye Can See

Normally the stool takes the form of little balls that are brownish or, if the animal eats grass and leaves, greenish in color. It does not have an unpleasant odor. Depending on what the animal has ingested, the stool will contain hair, teeth, claws, chitin, plant fibers, and not infrequently, sand and little rocks.

Symptoms of disease:
• If the stool is pasty or liquid in consistency and has a penetrating odor, this may be due to a change in diet. It may also be caused by inflammation in the digestive tract, however.
• If the stool contains blood, that points to some kind of intestinal lesion.

Treatment: Collect fresh stool samples and take or send them quickly to your veterinarian.

Inflammations in the Digestive Tract

Symptoms: Considerable decrease in activity, refusal to eat, pasty and foul-smelling stool, reddened or soiled cloaca. Infections are caused by bacteria or viruses and promoted by improper living conditions.

Treatment: After obtaining the results of a stool exam, the veterinarian will begin specific treatment.

Important: Since visible symptoms often appear relatively late, contact the veterinarian without delay.

Endoparasites

Symptoms: Apart from worms, which will be visible in fresh feces if

The veiled chameleon is easier to keep than other chameleon species.

the infestation is severe, you will not notice any of the large number of possible endoparasites. Nonetheless, they can cause emaciation, poisoning, and inflammation in the digestive tract.

Treatment: After the veterinarian establishes proof of the presence of endoparasites, appropriate medications will be prescribed.

Mites

Symptoms: Whitish-gray deposits on the skin of reptiles will indicate a mite infestation before you actually spot these blackish parasites, which are barely the size of a pinhead.

Mites feed on the blood of the host animal, preferring to perforate the soft areas of skin under the scales. General debilitation and stress results from the constant itching.

Treatment: If you detect an infestation when you purchase an animal (see External Parasites, page 30), dip the bag in which you carried it into a two percent solution of Nix, a brand-name product which is used to kill human hair lice. Place the animal in the wet bag for several hours. If you detect a mite infestation in your terrarium, spray the animals and the entire container thoroughly with the solution. Use as fine a spray as possible.

Caution: Don't treat reptiles with relatively large skin lesions and geckos with the solution. Instead, hang up one-inch squares of No-Pest strip, available in pet stores. Leave the piece in place for a few days, then remove them. Remove the water dish in the enclosure in which you have the insecticide pieces in place; replace the water dish after you take the insecticide out.

Ticks

Symptoms: Ticks, which can reach a size of 3 mm, are very flat-bodied

arthropods. They sink their jaws into soft areas of skin and underneath the scales and suck blood.

Treatment: Follow the treatment for mite infestations. If the extent of the skin damage makes it impossible to use Nix, rubbing cod-liver ointment on the affected areas will achieve good long-term results.

My tip: Since the ointment will get the terrarium messy, it is better to treat the animal in a quarantine terrarium.

External Injuries

Example: Bites, contused wounds, broken-off tail, crushed toe.

Treatment: If the injuries are minor, they can be treated with antibiotics or sulfonamide, in either powder or ointment form. Don't apply Band-Aids or dressings. Keep the animal in the quarantine terrarium, in conditions as sterile as possible. For more serious injuries, see the veterinarian.

Mouth Rot

Symptoms: Deposit of solidified mucus, abscesses, decay of tissue in the gum area and in the mouth.

Treatment: Dab with tincture of chamomile. Go to veterinarian.

My tip: To improve resistance, administer a multivitamin preparation, in accordance with manufacturer's directions.

Ulcers on the Skin

Symptoms: Abscesses in the skin ranging from pinhead size to penny size, frequently caused by metabolic disturbances.

Treatment: The veterinarian will lance the abscesses, clean the area around the wound, and prescribe a course of treatment.

My tip: Make sure the animals are adequately supplied with vitamins and are exposed to UV-A rays regularly.

Not all animals live to a ripe old age in a terrarium. Land turtles, however, can live over 50 years, large snakes at least 40 years, green iguanas 25 years and more; chameleons live only two to three years.

Skin Fungi in Reptiles

Symptoms: Formation of scabs on the skin, sometimes also suffused with blood, generally unaccompanied by formation of pus, caused by skin fungi (dermatophytes), which usually are promoted by excessive humidity in the terrarium.

Treatment: The veterinarian will take a tissue sample and try to prescribe an effective medication.

Note: The treatment is protracted.

Fungous Growths on the Skin

Symptoms: White, cottony deposits, occasionally including lesions suffused with blood. This disease usually results from dirty living conditions and another, frequently unrecognized, skin disease affecting amphibians that live in water.

Treatment: Administer preparations designed to combat fungous growth in ornamental fish, in accordance with manufacturer's directions.

Pneumonia (Inflammation of the Lungs)

Symptoms: Noticeable decrease in activity, refusal to eat, foam around the nostrils, jerky opening and shutting of mouth, breathing usually accompanied by clearly audible rattle. Infection promoted by inadequate control of temperature and humidity, for example, insufficient drop in nighttime temperature.

Treatment: The infection is treated by the veterinarian with antibiotics or sulfa drugs.

My tip: Build up resistance with vitamin doses.

Eye Inflammations, Swelling of the Eyelids

Symptoms: Reddening of the eye and noticeable swelling of the lids. Vitamin deficiency, as well as poor

A cardboard box is a good container in which to transport turtles and other reptiles.

terrarium hygiene, can be the cause. If only one lid is swollen, the animal probably has an injury.

Treatment: The veterinarian will prescribe eye drops for an inflammation and inject vitamins for swollen eyelids. As a supportive measure, give the animal a multivitamin preparation daily for at least four weeks, following the manufacturer's directions for use.

Metabolic Bone Disease

Symptoms: Curvature of the spine, the limbs, the tail, and the jaw. In turtles, the shell softens. Softening of the bones caused by insufficient deposit of calcium in the skeleton. Causes include inadequate exposure to UV rays, not enough vitamins and minerals, individual metabolic disturbances, and overfeeding of animals kept too warm in too small a space.

Treatment: Immediate veterinary care, high doses of calcium and multivitamins.

Index

Resources

Useful Addresses
Northern Ohio Association of
Herpetologists (NOAH)
Department of Biology
Case Western Reserve
University
Cleveland, OH 44106

Chicago Herpetological Society
2001 Clark Street
Chicago, IL 60614

Herpetologist's League
c/o Texas Natural Heritage
Program
Texas Parks and Wildlife
Department
Smith School Road
Austin, TX 78744

Society for the Study of
Amphibians and Reptiles
Department of Zoology
Miami University
Oxford, OH 45056

Books for
Further Reading
Bartlett, Richard
D. *Digest for
the Successful
Terrarium.* Morris
Plains, NJ: Terra-
Tetrafauna, 1989.

de Vosjoli, Philippe.
*Design and Main-
tenance of Desert
Vivaria.* Santee, CA:
Advanced Vivarium
Systems, 1996.

Zimmerman, E. *Breeding
Terrarium Animals.* Morris
Plains, NJ: T.F.H., 1986.

Periodicals
Reptiles
P.O. Box 6050
Mission Viejo, CA 92690

*Reptile and Amphibian
Magazine*
RD3 Box 3709
Pottsville, PA 17901

Reptile Hobbyist
One TFH Plaza
Neptune City, NJ 07753

The Vivarium
P.O. Box 3000067
Escondido, CA 92030

The Photos
Cramm: pages 32 above
right, 40, 52; Dossenbach: page
20 below left; Hoppe: page
64/inside back cover; Kahl:
inside front cover, pages 4, 5,
29, 32 above left, 33 above left,
center, 37 below; Karbe: pages
20 above left, 56; Koenig:
pages 20 above center, 25, 32
below left, below right, 33
below, 41, 44, 45; Lange: page
28; Nieuwenhuizen: page 49;
Bilder Pur/Okapia/McDonald:
page 57; Reinhard: front cover,
pages 9, 12, 17, 20 below right,
21 (all), 37 above, center, 53,
back cover; Schrempp: page 20
above right; Ziehm: pages 8, 33
above right.

The Cover Photos
Front cover: Leopard gecko
Back cover: Crevice spiny
lizard

Acknowledgments
The author and the publisher
wish to thank Dr. Ekkehard
Wolff of Munich's Hellabrunn
Zoo for his critical review of
the chapter on diseases and
attorney Reinhard Hahn for his
advice on legal issues.

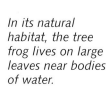

*In its natural
habitat, the tree
frog lives on large
leaves near bodies
of water.*

Important Notes

This guide book deals with the setting up of terrariums and the keeping of terrarium animals. All electrical appliances must have been tested and must bear the UL symbol. Lamps used in the area that can be affected by water from the terrarium must be guaranteed to be splashproof. Devices used under water must be designed for that purpose. Always unplug the devices when you are working near or with water. If your home's wiring is not yet equipped with a central fault current breaker, we recommend purchasing a surge protector usable in any wall socket.

When dealing with terrarium animals and food animals, follow the rules of good hygiene closely. The spines or juices of many terrarium plants can injure your skin, mucous membranes, and eyes. Clean your hands thoroughly every time you come in contact with animals and plants. Immediately rinse off any liquids that splash onto your face, and be sure children are informed about these procedures. If injuries occur, see your physician. When working with stones, wear protective goggles and work gloves. If you make rocks from synthetic materials, follow the manufacturers' directions carefully.

About the Author

For 26 years Harald Jes was director of Germany's Cologne Zoo's Aquarium, the building and development of which he contributed to substantially. He has dealt with the keeping of amphibians and reptiles for over 40 years. His special interest is the breeding of these animals. His professional duties also included training and evaluating zookeepers and master zookeepers.

About the Illustrator

György Jankovics is a trained graphic artist. He studied at the academies of art in Budapest and Hamburg. He draws animal and plant subjects for a number of well-respected publishing houses. He has illustrated a great many titles in Barron's series of nature books as well.

English translation © Copyright 1998 by Barron's Educational Series, Inc.

© 1996 by Gräfe und Unzer Verlag GmbH, München

Published originally under the title *Das Terrarium*

All inquiries should be addressed to:
Barron's Educational Series, Inc.
250 Wireless Boulevard
Hauppauge, New York 11788
http://www.barronseduc.com

Library of Congress Catalog Card No. 98-71616

International Standard Book Number 0-7641-0564-7

Printed in Hong Kong

9 8 7 6 5 4 3 2 1

Bearded drag-
ons grow
up to 22 inches
(55 cm) long
and are native
to Australia.
They like living
in a desert terrar-
ium decorated
with a sandy
floor, stones,
and branches,
on which they
enjoy climbing
and resting.